MASTERING WOODWORKING™

MAKING JOINTS

MASTERING WOODWORKING™

MAKING JOINTS

Techniques, Tips, and Problem-Solving Tricks

IAN J. KIRBY with JOHN KELSEY

Rodale Press, Inc.
Emmaus, Pennsylvania

OUR MISSION

We publish books that empower people's lives.

RODALE BOOKS

The authors and editors who compiled this book have tried to make all of the contents as accurate and as correct as possible. Plans, illustrations, photographs, and text have all been carefully checked and cross-checked. However, due to the variability of local conditions, construction materials, personal skill, and so on, neither the authors nor Rodale Press assumes any responsibility for any injuries suffered or for damages or other losses incurred that result from the material presented herein. All instructions and plans should be carefully studied and clearly understood before beginning construction.

Printed in the United States of America on acid-free ∞ , recycled ♻ paper

Mastering Woodworking: Making Joints Editorial Staff

Editor: Ken Burton
Project Writers: Ken Burton and Tony O'Malley
Book Designer: Jan Melchior
Illustrator: Glenn Hughes
Cover Photographer: John Hamel
Interior Photographer: Mitch Mandel
Interior Photo Stylist: Marianne Grape Laubach
Technical Artist: Dale Mack
Copy Editor: Carolyn Mandarano
Manufacturing Coordinator: Melinda B. Rizzo
Indexer: Nan N. Badgett
Editorial Assistance: Nancy Kutches and
    Stephanie Wenner

On the cover: Making box joints on the router
    table (page 84)

Rodale Home and Garden Books

Vice President and Editorial Director:
    Margaret Lydic Balitas
Managing Editor, Woodworking and DIY Books:
    Kevin Ireland
Art Director: Michael Mandarano
Associate Art Director: Mary Ellen Fanelli
Studio Manager: Leslie Keefe
Copy Director: Dolores Plikaitis
Production Manager: Helen Clogston
Office Manager: Karen Earl-Braymer
Project Designers:
    Ken Burton: Garden Bench
    Ian J. Kirby: Side Table
    Tony O'Malley: Gear Box and Study Desk
Rodale Press Design Shop staff:
    Phil Gehret
    Fred Matlack

If you have any questions or comments concerning the editorial content of this book, please write to:
    Rodale Press, Inc.
    Book Readers' Service
    33 East Minor Street
    Emmaus, PA 18098

Library of Congress Cataloging-in-Publication Data

Kirby, Ian J., date
    Mastering woodworking. Making joints / Ian J. Kirby with John Kelsey.
        p. cm.
    Includes index.
    ISBN 0–87596–745–0 (hardcover : alk. paper)
    1. Woodwork—Amateurs' manuals. 2. Joinery—Amateurs' manuals. I. Kelsey, John II. Title III. Series: Mastering woodworking.
TT185.K376 1996
684'.08—dc20   96–2621

Distributed in the book trade by St. Martin's Press

2 4 6 8 10 9 7 5 3 1 hardcover

ABOUT IAN KIRBY
AND JOHN KELSEY

Ian Kirby learned woodworking from Edward Barnsley, the last of England's great Arts-and-Crafts designer-makers. He studied furniture design at Leeds School of Design, Hull College of Technology, and the London School of Furniture. Kirby came to the United States in 1976 to open his own studio-atelier. Since then, he has been invited to teach woodworking in schools across the country. Lately, he has been working as an independent designer, furniture maker, architectural woodworker, and writer. Kirby lives in Milford, Connecticut.

Coauthor John Kelsey is a journalist and amateur woodworker. From 1976 until 1984, he was the editor of *Fine Woodworking* magazine. He has edited many books and writes frequently about woodworking and furniture design. In 1994, Kelsey founded Cambium Press, an independent publisher specializing in the practical and decorative arts. He lives in Newtown, Connecticut.

Contents

Projects

INTRODUCTION

You can always spot a wood-worker at a party. He's the guy down on his hands and knees peering up at the underside of the coffee table trying to figure out how it was made. I've embarrassed my wife terribly doing things like that. But I know I'm not the only one who does it.

I exhibited a small writing desk in a local craft show some years ago. During the opening reception, I was talking to the show's organizer about the joinery and about how I had shaped the legs. When he asked about a mortise I'd cut on the inside of the back apron, up behind the drawer, I knew he had to be a woodworker. Who else would have crawled under there to find this joint? He confessed, and we had a good chuckle over this peculiar habit.

Much to my wife's dismay, however, I'm not likely to quit peering under tables and opening the odd drawer. There's just too much to gain from looking at the way other woodworkers have done things.

That's one of the underlying premises of this book. It was designed and written for wood-workers of all experience levels,

with the idea that there's always something more to learn. If you are just starting out, I suggest you start at the beginning of this book. Taken in sequence, the chapters will walk you through the entire joinery process, providing information about the way joints are made. You'll come to see that once you've mastered a handful of skills, there is not a joint you won't be able to cut.

If you have a little more experience, you may want to use the book more as a reference. Turn to either the table of contents or the index to help you navigate, then dive right into the techniques for cutting the joints you need. Even if you know your way around the shop pretty well, I'm sure you'll find tricks in here that you may not have thought of before. I know I did.

Once you get into the real nitty-gritty, step-by-step, how-to sequences, you'll discover several elements that can help you get the job done right. First off, the text and the accompanying photos and illustrations show you exactly how to proceed, from the initial layout to clamping the joint home. Along with these instructions, you'll find:

- "Troubleshooting" boxes, which point out potential pitfalls and how to avoid them;
- "Problem Solving" sidebars, which help get you out of many of the most common woes;
- "Rippings," which offer helpful tips and tricks; and
- "Fact or Fiction" boxes, which debunk common misconceptions about woodworking techniques.

And if you're looking for an extra challenge, check out the techniques labeled "Pushing the Limits." These may inspire you to try something a little out of the ordinary—something that may elevate your woodworking to another level of sophistication.

Finally, at the back of the book, you'll find complete plans for four projects that put the techniques discussed up front to practical use. Build the projects included as they are, or simply refer to them to see how the various joints were used—almost as good as a quick peek under your friend's new curio cabinet.

Ken Burton
Editor

TECHNIQUES

1

INTRODUCTION TO JOINERY

Key Ingredients

Joinery is the process of connecting two or more pieces of wood in order to achieve both aesthetic and structural design goals. The physical nature of wood is the reason for making joints the way we do: Wood is a fibrous material with grain direction that shrinks and expands with changes in atmospheric moisture. The whole universe of woodworking joints has evolved in response to wood and the way it behaves.

A joint is the area where two or more pieces of wood come together.

Generally the pieces are shaped to fit one another and are usually anchored by glue. The key to joint making is accuracy because success depends on the mating parts fitting closely together. This is true whether you work with hand tools, machines, or both together, as I do.

Joint making is a means to an end, not an end in itself, as explained in *The Woodworking Process.* Yet it is easy to get lost in the technical challenge of cutting perfect joints and to lose sight of the objective—a beautiful and useful item made out of wood.

Joint making isn't a rigid canon

of historical lore handed down from our grandfathers either. It's an evolving craft driven by changes in materials, tools and technologies, and our aesthetic sensibilities.

Materials

The wood we buy today is not the same wood our grandfathers enjoyed working. All of the big trees are gone, and second-growth forests are rarely given time to approach the size of old growth. Some species—elm and chestnut, for example—have been afflicted with disease and have died out. Other species—red alder and

In years gone by, the finest furniture, like this cellaret (left), had no visible evidence of how the pieces were fastened together. In contrast, today's craftsmen often leave the joinery exposed (right), as visible evidence of the maker's hand.

Oregon maple, for example—have come to market. International trade in exotic timbers is subject not only to tropical deforestation but also to political pressures. Even where they still exist, many species rarely reach the marketplace in the form of logs or planks and instead are available only as veneers and manufactured parts.

On the other hand, commercial wood today is more uniformly seasoned and graded than it was a couple of generations ago. You can't get wide planks any longer, but you can get better-seasoned material, well suited to our atmospherically controlled interiors.

Tools and Technologies

It's easy to forget that the antique furniture we admire was gotten out of the log without the help of electricity. Water-powered sash saws have been around since about the fourteenth century, but planing wood flat and smooth was hard hand labor until about a hundred years ago. Woodworking machinery--especially the table saw and the high-speed router, which have also completely changed the way we design and cut joints--has increased our ability to produce. The biscuit joiner has given us an entirely new kind of joint. Modern measuring tools—the engineer's combination square and dial caliper, in particular—offer new insight into accuracy.

You can still make every kind of furniture and most (not all) kinds of joints using hand tools alone. In fact, there is a great deal of personal satisfaction in learning how to use these tools and a certain freedom from the limitations imposed by machines. But there is no magical purity in the results of one method or the other.

No one can tell by observing a mortise-and-tenon joint whether it was made with hand tools or by machine, nor is one joint stronger or better than the other. However, you'll find the greatest freedom as a woodworker when you can move from machines to hand methods at will, using whichever approach best suits the situation at hand.

Aesthetics

Before machine production, a hidden connection and a lustrous surface were wondrous things. High style demanded that all joinery, and even end grain, be hidden. A visible joint was a mark of crude, utilitarian work.

Industrial production, and its ability to reproduce uniform parts, has inverted our sense of aesthetics. People are likely to see exposed joinery as evidence of real craftsmanship, even though the blind, or concealed, version of the same joint might be more difficult to make.

An exposed joint can add highlight and shadow or pattern to a form. It can help the viewer understand the architecture of the piece by revealing the relationship of intersecting parts. Exposed joinery also offers an opportunity to add rich detail, which can be a source of delight as people touch and use the object.

Of course, this isn't to say that exposed joinery is necessary or even appropriate in all situations. Visible joints lend a piece a certain aesthetic of its own that may not be in keeping with the overall look. You should view exposed joinery as an option, one of many design elements that you can throw into the mix as you're planning what you want your project to look like.

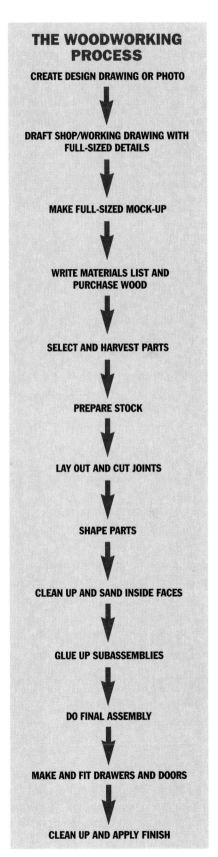

THE WOODWORKING PROCESS

CREATE DESIGN DRAWING OR PHOTO

↓

DRAFT SHOP/WORKING DRAWING WITH FULL-SIZED DETAILS

↓

MAKE FULL-SIZED MOCK-UP

↓

WRITE MATERIALS LIST AND PURCHASE WOOD

↓

SELECT AND HARVEST PARTS

↓

PREPARE STOCK

↓

LAY OUT AND CUT JOINTS

↓

SHAPE PARTS

↓

CLEAN UP AND SAND INSIDE FACES

↓

GLUE UP SUBASSEMBLIES

↓

DO FINAL ASSEMBLY

↓

MAKE AND FIT DRAWERS AND DOORS

↓

CLEAN UP AND APPLY FINISH

Understanding Grain Direction

Wood comes from trees. It's fibrous, it has a structure, and it is not the same in every direction. Although these assertions may seem trivial, they are the organizational basis for all wood-working and also for this book.

Where Figure Comes From shows how boards come out of the trunk of a tree. The long, fibrous cells that give wood its bulk and strength grow in the same direction as the tree trunk. This is referred to as the wood's grain direction. The tree grows by adding a new layer of wood to its outside surface every year. The long fibers accumulate in distinct annual rings, which you can see on the cut trunk of the tree and on the end-grain surface of a board.

When you cut along the grain, the result is a long-grain surface. Long-grain surfaces can be glued together. When you cut across the grain, the result is an end-grain, or cross-grain, surface. End-grain sur-

WHERE FIGURE COMES FROM

Quarter-sawn wood is cut on a radius. It shows straight, even grain, called radial figure. It also exposes the ray tissue, which appears as silvery flashes in wood like oak.

Rift-sawn wood comes from cutting near the center of the tree, but not on it. A rift-sawn plank may show elements of both radial and tangential figure.

LONG GRAIN

END GRAIN

Flat-sawn wood comes from sawing through the tree trunk away from the center. It shows the vees and whorls of tangential grain, called cathedral figure.

faces do not accept glue well and cannot be glued together directly or to long-grain surfaces.

Wood Movement

Wood moves when the amount of moisture in the atmosphere changes. As humidity levels rise,

the wood takes on moisture and swells. When humidity levels drop, wood loses moisture and shrinks. This is illustrated in *Wood Movement*.

However, because of its internal structure, wood doesn't move uniformly. It hardly changes in length, it changes somewhat in the radial direction, and it changes considerably in the tangential direction (about twice that of the radial direction). The difference between radial and tangential movement, called the shrinkage differential, is the reason that wood distorts as it dries.

Joinery and Grain Direction

All of the methods of joining wood are responses to the grain structure of wood and the way it moves. As shown in *Joinery Configurations*, there are three fundamental ways boards come together.

WOOD MOVEMENT

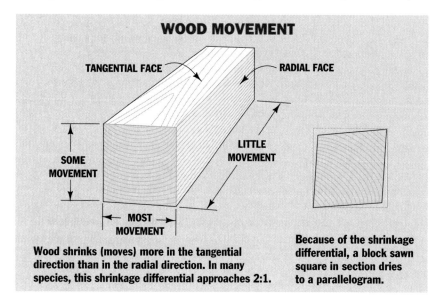

TANGENTIAL FACE

RADIAL FACE

SOME MOVEMENT

LITTLE MOVEMENT

MOST MOVEMENT

Wood shrinks (moves) more in the tangential direction than in the radial direction. In many species, this shrinkage differential approaches 2:1.

Because of the shrinkage differential, a block sawn square in section dries to a parallelogram.

RIPPINGS

BALANCE EQUALS STRENGTH
How strong does a joint have to be? Most of the time, you can avoid weakness and resolve structural problems by balancing the amount of wood tissue between the two parts of the joint. Of the total amount of wood involved in the joint, half should come from one piece and half from the other. This way there is no weak link.

- **Edge grain to edge grain (or face grain to face grain).** Edge joints make wood wider or thicker or both. Since the grain structure is parallel, two similar pieces of edge-joined wood probably will stay together with moisture content changes. See Chapter 3, beginning on page 20.
- **End-grain to long-grain rail joints.** Rail joints, such as the mortise and tenon, make frames and constructions like table leg and apron assemblies. In most situations, one piece is cross grain to the other, and moisture-induced conflict is inevitable. You can control this conflict by making joints that involve relatively small sections of wood. See Chapter 4, beginning on page 42, and Chapter 5, beginning on page 60.
- **End-grain to long-grain carcase joints.** Carcase joints, primarily the dovetail, make boxes. These joints, which have no cross-grain conflict, are covered in depth in Chapter 6, beginning on page 80.

The frame-and-panel assembly is so important to woodworking that it belongs in this overview. It consists of a thin, stable frame surrounding a free-moving panel. The result is the basis for many kinds of furniture.

Which Joint to Make?

Choosing which joint to make is a complex decision. Here are some questions that should point you in the right direction:

- What is the grain direction of the parts you intend to connect? You need to know where you can achieve long-grain to long-grain gluing area, since this is what holds wood joints together.
- What are the visual requirements of the design? Do you want to see exposed elements of wood joints, such as dovetail pins and through tenons? Do you want the joint to be concealed so that it's not a factor in the visual composition?

By keeping the answers to these questions in mind, you can proceed to choose and design a system of joinery that should last a lifetime.

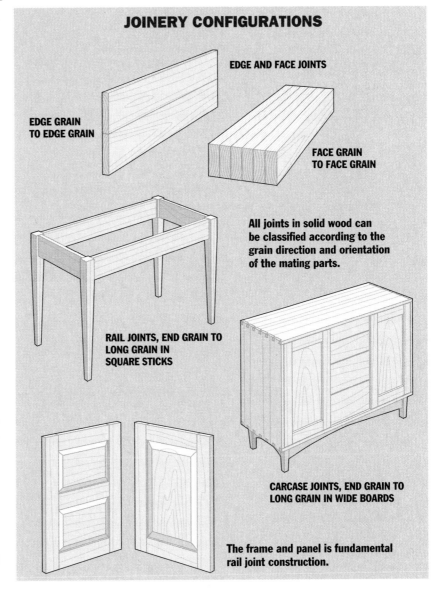

JOINERY CONFIGURATIONS

EDGE AND FACE JOINTS

EDGE GRAIN TO EDGE GRAIN

FACE GRAIN TO FACE GRAIN

All joints in solid wood can be classified according to the grain direction and orientation of the mating parts.

RAIL JOINTS, END GRAIN TO LONG GRAIN IN SQUARE STICKS

CARCASE JOINTS, END GRAIN TO LONG GRAIN IN WIDE BOARDS

The frame and panel is fundamental rail joint construction.

Buying and Storing Wood

When it comes to hardwood, there's no such thing as a deal. You'll get what you pay for. Life is too short to waste time struggling with lousy materials, so for furniture making, I always buy the best wood I can find.

At the same time, you won't find affordable hardwood at your local home center, and you probably won't like the prices at a full-service lumberyard either. You have to be creative and persistent in your search. One source might be a large local hardwood user who will sell to you directly. For example, I get a lot of my material from a specialty flooring manufacturer who buys huge quantities of premium wood. He sells me his stray boards of curly figure or bird's-eye, which would be distracting in a floor.

You may be able to buy through a local cabinet shop, millwork shop, or kitchen builder. If a shop is buying hardwood in lots of 1,000 board feet, the owner may be willing to add 200 board feet to his next order for you or to sell you stock out of his own inventory.

Also, if there's a woodworking club or guild in your area, join up. Its members almost certainly will have tracked down the local sources.

When you want to use premium cuts, such as wide walnut slabs or imported woods, you'll have to travel to a specialty dealer's yard, or you'll have to trust one of the mail-order specialty wood firms. You'll find that a knowledgeable salesman can be your best ally. If you can explain what you are trying to do, he'll probably be able to find the

Store boards flat, in stickered piles. The stickers allow air to circulate around every surface so that the wood can adjust to local conditions. Stickers should be ¾ inch square and spaced 16 to 24 inches apart.

material you need. A reputable dealer will also accept returns.

How Much Wood to Buy?

The worst thing (next to cutting off your hand) is running out of wood in the middle of a project, so

RIPPINGS

MEASURING MOISTURE

A battery-powered moisture meter is the only practical, reliable way to measure the moisture content of wood. A typical meter costs about $150—cheap insurance compared to the loss of making a complex piece of furniture from improperly seasoned wood. This type of meter has two sharp electrodes, which you drive into the wood along the grain. The meter works by measuring the electrical resistance between the electrodes. The resistance drops as the moisture content increases.

it pays to carefully think out what you'll need before you buy, as shown in *Planning Your Purchase.* When I can select the wood before I buy it, I generally get 25 percent more than what's called for in my bill of materials. This gives me enough extra to work around defects and to make a couple of additional parts.

When you're ordering by mail or piggybacking your wood order onto someone else's, you won't be able to select your material in advance. In this case, I buy twice the amount called for in my bill of materials, if I can afford it. This gives me enough to select the best wood for my current project, and it leaves some extra for the next one.

Although I don't attempt to keep an inventory of hardwood, I always have a stash of service materials in the shop. These materials are for jigs, fixtures, and interior parts of cabinets. I generally have about 100 board feet of a white wood such as poplar or soft maple, the same amount of pine, and several thicknesses of maple or birch plywood, medium-density fiberboard (MDF), particleboard, and Masonite.

If you have a small shop, where storage space is at a premium, I'd still try to keep at least a half-sheet of plywood or MDF and a few pine boards on hand.

Storing Your Stock

In earlier times, when all wood was air dried, craftsmen had to buy wood ahead and store it in their own sheds for a couple of years because this was the only way to get control of the wood's moisture content. Moisture content is the weight of water in a piece of wood, expressed as a percentage of the dry weight of the wood. For example, a green board might weigh 100 pounds at the sawmill and 50 pounds if you were to oven dry all of the moisture out of it. The moisture content of the green board would be 100 percent, and the dry board would have 0 percent moisture.

After a board has been oven dried, it will pick up moisture from the atmosphere until the moisture content of the board reaches an equilibrium with atmospheric humidity. In most parts of North America, wood settles at around 8 percent moisture content.

Today, most hardwood lumber is kiln dried by a processor and carefully stored by a dealer. You can generally rely on hardwood having been dried to 7 or 8 percent moisture content. It will then gain or lose a small amount of moisture, depending on how it's been transported and stored. This means you don't have to store several years'

worth of wood, but you do need to have enough room to store the stock for your current project and to condition the wood to your own situation. Remember that wood never stops exchanging moisture with the atmosphere, and it gains and loses moisture from every surface, not just from the end grain. Here are some things to keep in mind as you're planning your work:

- If you buy kiln-dried wood, do the final conditioning by bringing the boards indoors, into heated space, for two to four weeks before you work with it. Several weeks of advance storage inside the house will make a big difference.
- If you buy air-dried wood directly from a local sawmill,

plan to store it for at least a year per inch of thickness (two years is better) before you work it.
- Don't attempt to make furniture from green, unseasoned wood unless you're willing to study the techniques and constructions that have been developed specifically to deal with it.
- Air dry and store boards flat, under a cover, and in stickered piles, as shown in the photo. The stickers permit air to circulate around every surface of the boards. If you prefer to store your wood standing on end, make sure it is vertical, or else you will induce bowing. And if the floor is concrete, put down a scrap plank first to serve as a moisture barrier.

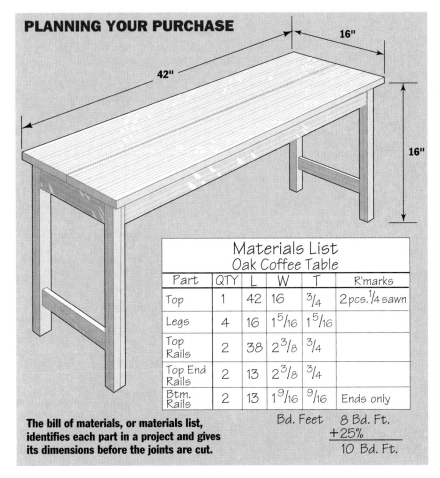

PLANNING YOUR PURCHASE

42"   16"   16"

Materials List Oak Coffee Table					
Part	QTY	L	W	T	R'marks
Top	1	42	16	$^3/_4$	2 pcs. $^1/_4$ sawn
Legs	4	16	$1^5/_{16}$	$1^5/_{16}$	
Top Rails	2	38	$2^3/_8$	$^3/_4$	
Top End Rails	2	13	$2^3/_8$	$^3/_4$	
Btm. Rails	2	13	$1^9/_{16}$	$^9/_{16}$	Ends only

Bd. Feet   8 Bd. Ft.
+25%
10 Bd. Ft.

The bill of materials, or materials list, identifies each part in a project and gives its dimensions before the joints are cut.

Selecting Wood

After you've acquired your stack of wood, the next step is to select the pieces for your project.

When factory workers process wood into parts and panels, they can't afford the time to select it for figure or grain direction. But you can. As an individual craftsman, you have the luxury—and in my opinion, the obligation—to select your wood with care and taste. You're able to take the time to go through the available boards and decide which one to use where, and you can spend as much time at it as you like. On any worthwhile project, I expect to spend a lot of time on selection—studying the wood, sorting where I'll use it, and then studying it some more. I like to stand the wood for my current work on end, along the shop wall, where I can see it and think about how best to use it.

Selection is a very important step in woodworking. It's a process, it takes time, and it's done with a piece of chalk, not with a saw. Go at it like this:

- If the wood is still rough, begin by jointing one face and planing the other to the maximum thickness the wood will yield so you can really see how it looks.
- With your bill of materials in hand, go over the boards with a tape measure, chalk, and chalkline, and mark out the pieces you want. Mark all of the pieces you need for your project, as shown in the photo.
- For good furniture, eliminate all knots, checks, and other defects, such as those shown in *Warped Wood* and *Laying Out Parts*. It's often tempting to save wood by

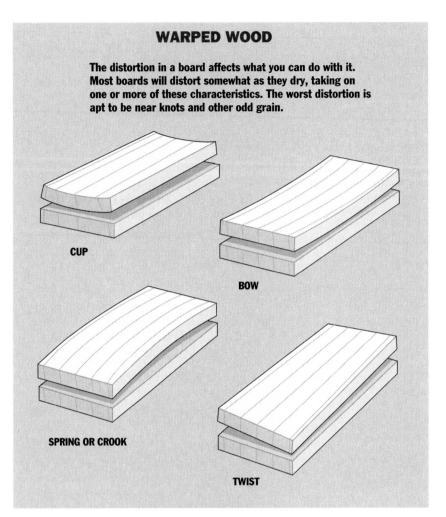

WARPED WOOD

The distortion in a board affects what you can do with it. Most boards will distort somewhat as they dry, taking on one or more of these characteristics. The worst distortion is apt to be near knots and other odd grain.

CUP

BOW

SPRING OR CROOK

TWIST

Chalk your workpieces onto the boards. Chalk wipes off with a damp rag, so it's easy to re-mark your pieces if you change your mind.

cutting close to a knot, but the grain of the wood is liable to be distorted for some distance. You can't cut good joints in distorted grain, so mark your crosscuts to avoid it.

- Mark wide boards that contain the pith of the tree or that were cut just to one side of the pith for ripping into narrower pieces. These boards are liable to be severely cupped and distorted.

- Sight the board like a rifle to see if it is distorted. Boards that wind or twist may be fine when crosscut into shorter lengths.

- Don't be seduced by straight edges. If the grain of the wood runs diagonally across the board, lay out your parts on the diagonal.

- If you change your mind, wipe off the chalk with a damp rag, and re-mark your pieces until you get everything the way you want it.

Harvesting the Pieces

With your boards marked, you're ready to cut them up to harvest your selections. You can use a handsaw, a table saw, a band saw, a portable circular saw, or a jigsaw. There's no set method of harvesting, but in general, it's easier to crosscut boards first, then rip them. Harvest your pieces oversized, by at least ½ inch in length and the same or less in width, depending on whether the board is bowed or cupped. Harvest all of the wood you need for your project, then stack the pieces with stickers in between, much as you would with a stack of boards.

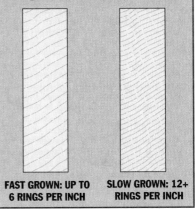

RIPPINGS

THE STRONGEST WOOD
In softwoods, the strongest wood is slow grown, with the annual rings spaced closely together. However, in hardwoods, the situation is the reverse, and fast-grown wood, with wide annual rings, is stronger than slow-grown wood.

FAST GROWN: UP TO 6 RINGS PER INCH   SLOW GROWN: 12+ RINGS PER INCH

LAYING OUT PARTS
Select the figure and grain structure you want from each board.

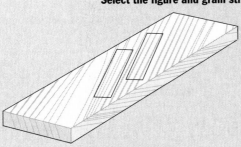

Don't let the board's edges dictate how your pieces look. Cut pieces so the grain aligns with their edges, not the board's.

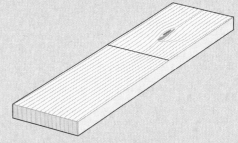

Cut well back from knots, or position knots in the center of a piece, away from the joinery.

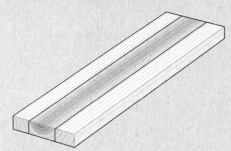

Avoid the pith of the tree, as it distorts badly.

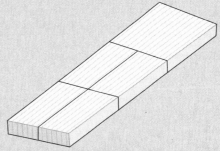

Severely warped boards can often be used when cut into short and/or narrow pieces.

2

PREPARING STOCK FOR JOINERY

Key Ingredients

Stock preparation is the foundation of making joints and furniture. It's a sequential process that can't be short-circuited. It begins when you select your wood, and it ends when every piece in your project has been cut flat, square, and precisely the right size. Believe it or not, when you're done preparing your stock, you'll be about at the halfway point in your project. The remaining tasks—cutting and fitting the joints, assembling, cleaning up, and finishing—are what we think of as "woodworking." But those tasks can't begin until stock preparation is complete.

The Preparation Sequence

Preparing stock is repetitive, hard work. You soon will establish a routine so you can move right through preparation and get down to the heart of your project. The complete preparation sequence is shown in *Stock Preparation*.

Measuring Tools

For joint making, you need good measuring tools like those shown in the photo. These include the following:

● **Straightedge.** A straightedge measures 180 degrees, which tells you flatness. It is absolutely

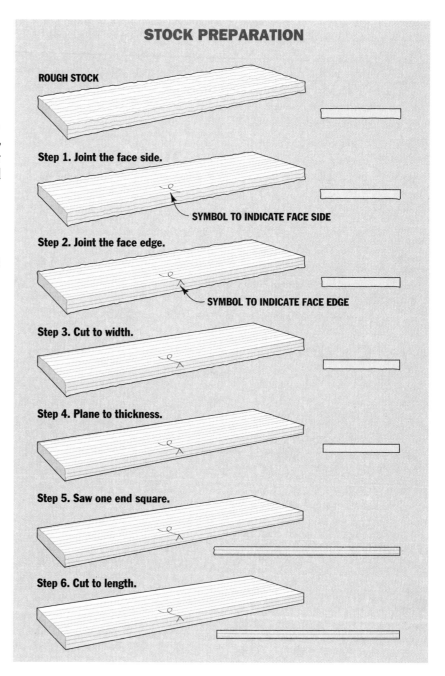

STOCK PREPARATION

ROUGH STOCK

Step 1. Joint the face side.

← SYMBOL TO INDICATE FACE SIDE

Step 2. Joint the face edge.

← SYMBOL TO INDICATE FACE EDGE

Step 3. Cut to width.

Step 4. Plane to thickness.

Step 5. Saw one end square.

Step 6. Cut to length.

vital to have a good straightedge. If you can afford it, I recommend an engineering-quality, steel, 24-inch-long straightedge.

- **Square.** A square, as shown in *Using a Square*, measures 90 degrees, which tells you squareness. The modern combination square, which is made entirely of metal, is more accurate than the traditional wooden-stock try square. The combination square has other uses, too: The sliding stock lets you set and transfer measurements and gauge depths. The basic square is 12 inches long; a 4- or 6-inch square is also useful.

- **Winding sticks.** Winding sticks measure flatness, or indicate twist, in an edge or surface. They are simply an identical pair of straight sticks, about 12 inches long, with parallel edges. The photos on page 12 show how to use them.

- **Steel rule and tape measure.** These tools measure dimensions and distances. A 3-foot steel rule marked in sixteenths or finer increments is most useful. For furniture making, it's much handier than a carpenter's folding rule.

- **Sliding bevel.** A sliding bevel transfers angles, which woodworkers establish by direct measurement, without regard to their value in degrees, as shown in *Setting a Bevel*. The metal bevel works better than the wooden version, and it costs less.

- **Dial caliper.** A dial caliper, another engineering tool, makes it easy to measure in hundredths of an inch, a degree of accuracy you can achieve with

standard woodworking tools. You don't need an expensive caliper. Even the plastic $25 version available at your local hardware store works.

- **Hand lens.** An 8x or 10x hand lens will show you what is happening to your tools and your work. Use it to inspect surfaces you've pared or machined, as well as to inspect your cutting tools. You'll be surprised at what you can learn about woodworking by looking through a hand lens.

No matter what you are doing, your measuring tools should be right at hand, ready to use.

USING A SQUARE

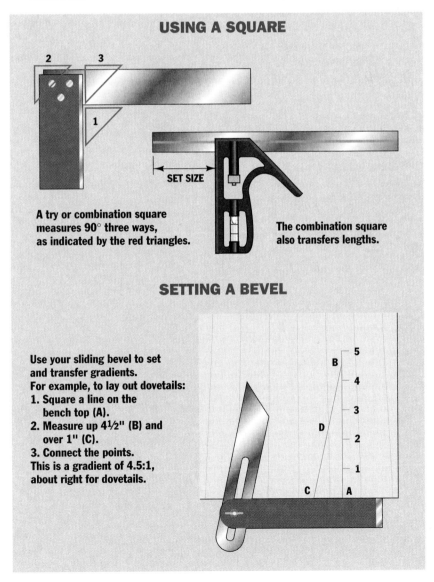

A try or combination square measures 90° three ways, as indicated by the red triangles.

SET SIZE

The combination square also transfers lengths.

SETTING A BEVEL

Use your sliding bevel to set and transfer gradients. For example, to lay out dovetails:
1. Square a line on the bench top (A).
2. Measure up 4½" (B) and over 1" (C).
3. Connect the points. This is a gradient of 4.5:1, about right for dovetails.

Jointing the Face Side

The face side is the reference from which you establish the face edge, and from these two surfaces follows everything else. A face side is:

- flat in length,
- flat in width,
- out of winding (not twisted).

Designating one side of a board as the face side doesn't have anything to do with which side looks better. The face side is simply the surface from which you measure and gauge. In most projects, the face side is the inside surface.

Joint the designated face according to the method laid out in "Jointer Technique" on pages 14–15. Then check your work. You need a long straightedge and a pair of winding sticks to gauge your face side. The last act in preparing the face side is to mark it with a pencil so you can keep track of it. The traditional mark is shown in *Checking the Face Edge.*

Note: If you have neither jointer nor planer, you can pay to have

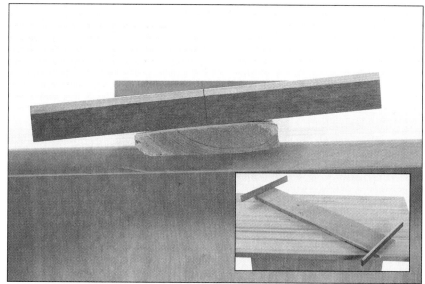

Set a winding stick at each end of your workpiece, and sight the top edge of the far stick over the top edge of the nearer one. If the sticks' edges don't line up, the surface of the workpiece is not flat.

your boards milled at a local woodworking shop. In most parts of the country, this millwork will cost you between $25 and $35 an hour, but a good shop should be able to mill between 50 and 100 board feet in that amount of time.

If you go to a mill, don't take raw planks. Instead, crosscut them to length, leaving a little extra for squaring up, and rip them to width if you can. This way, you'll end up with the thickest boards possible.

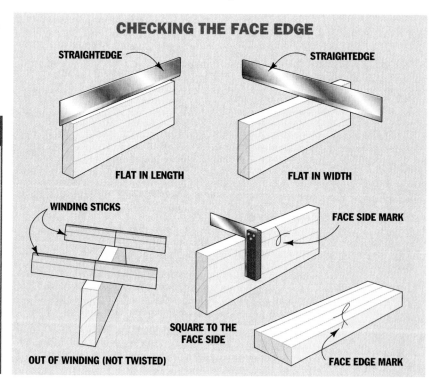

CHECKING THE FACE EDGE

STRAIGHTEDGE

STRAIGHTEDGE

FLAT IN LENGTH

FLAT IN WIDTH

WINDING STICKS

FACE SIDE MARK

SQUARE TO THE FACE SIDE

OUT OF WINDING (NOT TWISTED)

FACE EDGE MARK

Jointing the Face Edge

The next step is to prepare the face edge in relation to the face side. The face edge has four characteristics:

- flat in length,
- flat in width,
- out of winding (not twisted),
- square to the face side.

Joint the face edge, as shown in "Jointing Wood Flat and Square" on page 14. Then check the face edge, using a long straightedge, a pair of winding sticks, and a try square or combination square, as shown in *Checking the Face Edge*. When you have finished, mark the edge.

Router Jointing

If you don't have a jointer, or if a workpiece is too big for the one you do have, you can produce a straight edge with a router.

STEP 1 Rip the pieces as straight and as square as you can on the table saw.

STEP 2 Install a straight bit at least $\frac{1}{2}$ inch in diameter and at least as long as your board is thick.

STEP 3 Make a fence for your router table, like the one shown in *Jointing on the Router Table*, and set it so the outfeed side is tangent to the arc of the bit.

STEP 4 Pass the pieces by the bit from right to left.

To joint with a hand-held router, use the same bit as above and guide the router along a straightedge, as shown in *Jointing with a Hand-Held Router*.

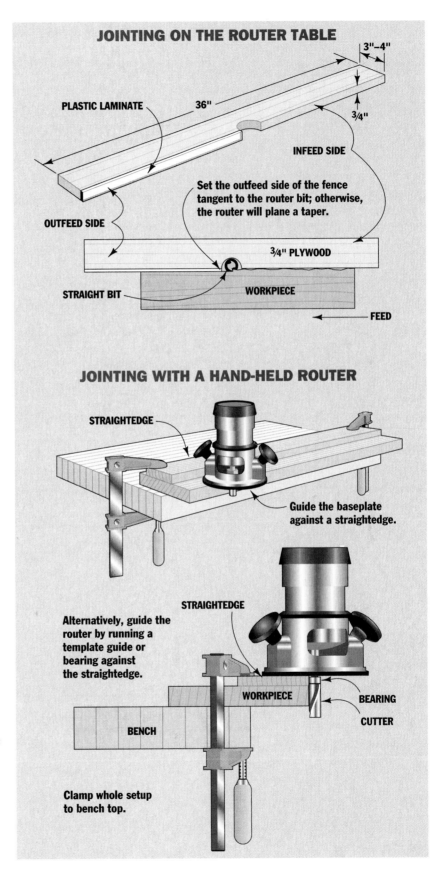

JOINTING ON THE ROUTER TABLE

PLASTIC LAMINATE 36" 3"–4" 3/4"

INFEED SIDE

Set the outfeed side of the fence tangent to the router bit; otherwise, the router will plane a taper.

OUTFEED SIDE

3/4" PLYWOOD

STRAIGHT BIT WORKPIECE

FEED

JOINTING WITH A HAND-HELD ROUTER

STRAIGHTEDGE

Guide the baseplate against a straightedge.

STRAIGHTEDGE

Alternatively, guide the router by running a template guide or bearing against the straightedge.

WORKPIECE BEARING CUTTER

BENCH

Clamp whole setup to bench top.

JOINTER TECHNIQUE

Jointing wood flat and square relies on a combination of good preparation and good technique. Start by making sure the knives are sharp and correctly set. Also, make sure the blade guard swings freely and closes over the knives.

"Jointing Wood Flat and Square" shows you the step-by-step technique for jointing.

Here are some other points to consider:
- You have to use your whole body to joint a flat surface. Stand alongside the jointer with your legs spread so that you're balanced and able to push.
- Hold the wood down on the table with the flat of your hand. For safety, never wrap your fingers over the edges of the board.

- Joint the concave side of a cupped board first, then use the two edges of the cup as a bearing surface.
- For a twisted board, place one hand in the center of the board and balance it as level as you can on the jointer's infeed table. Propel it over the jointer from its center to create two flat spots. Successive passes over the jointer will connect the flat areas.

STEP-BY-STEP: JOINTING WOOD FLAT AND SQUARE

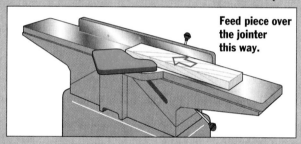

Feed piece over the jointer this way.

STEP 1 Read the grain direction on the edge of the board, and joint with it. A lot of tear-out means you're cutting the wrong way.

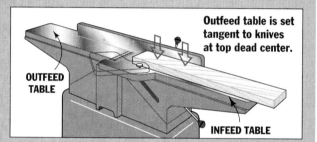

Outfeed table is set tangent to knives at top dead center.

OUTFEED TABLE

INFEED TABLE

STEP 2 Hold the board firmly on the infeed table as you start the cut, but not so hard that you distort it. Propel it with both hands.

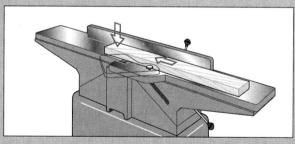

STEP 3 After 6 inches of the board has passed over the cutter, transfer your left hand to the outfeed side and press the board hard to the table.

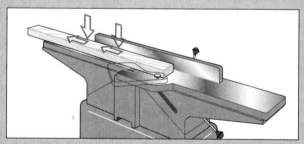

STEP 4 Once 24 inches has passed over the cutter, transfer your right hand to the outfeed side and pull/push the board past the cutter.

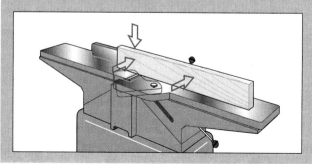

When jointing edges, press the face side of the workpiece tight to the fence. When the leading edge of the work has passed the cutterhead, begin to transfer pressure to the outfeed side of the fence. Check the workpiece for square after the cut, and adjust the fence if necessary.

TROUBLESHOOTING

JOINTING CLEAN, SMOOTH FACES AND EDGES

A sharp jointer makes shavings, not chips or dust. It leaves a cut surface. If you look at the surface of your workpiece with a magnifying glass, you'll be able to see whether the wood fibers have been cleanly cut or not. You may think you can get away with dull or poorly set knives, but they will pound and tear the wood fibers.

Then if you glue the resulting surface, the bond will be weak.

For a quick tune-up, you can sharpen the knives right in the machine, as shown in *Sharpening the Knives.* Large dings in the knives will require you to remove them from the machine and have them ground. "Setting the Knives" shows how to reset the knives so

they are all the same height.

If you know you are feeding slowly and smoothly, but you're still getting coarse, widely spaced knife marks, one knife is probably set higher than the others and doing all of the work. Find out by unplugging the machine and rotating the cutterhead by hand to see how far each knife moves a stick of wood.

SHARPENING THE KNIVES

Hold the stone at an angle, almost touching the cutterhead.

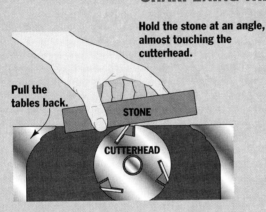

Pull the tables back.

STONE

CUTTERHEAD

TOP VIEW

Make circular strokes back and forth across the knife.

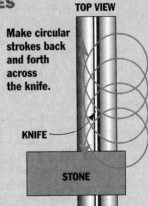

KNIFE

STONE

STEP-BY-STEP: SETTING THE KNIVES

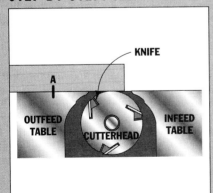

KNIFE

A

OUTFEED TABLE

CUTTERHEAD

INFEED TABLE

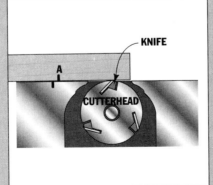

KNIFE

A

CUTTERHEAD

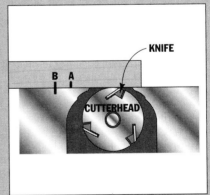

KNIFE

B A

CUTTERHEAD

STEP 1 Place a stick on the outfeed table and mark a line at A on the stick and across the table. Lower the tables so the stick barely clears the cutterhead.

STEP 2 Rotate the cutterhead so the knife picks up the stick. The knife will deposit the stick with the lines offset. Mark the stick from the line on the table.

STEP 3 Repeat with each knife. Starting at mark A, the stick should end at mark B. A shortfall indicates a low knife. An overshoot indicates a high knife.

Cutting to Width

To cut wood to width, put the face side down on the table saw table and guide the face edge against the rip fence. It's dangerous to use the table saw to cut stock to width until you have prepared a face side and a face edge—a piece that is warped and/or crooked is quite likely to bind with the blade and kick back. Saw to the finished width you need, plus 1/32 inch for cleaning up. For more information, see "Safe Ripping."

TROUBLESHOOTING

SAW BLADES FOR RIPPING

On a 10-inch table saw, use a 24- to 40-tooth carbide-tipped saw blade, with alternate-top-bevel configuration. A blade with more teeth is too fine for ripping and is liable to bog down.

If the table saw glazes or burns the cut surface, the teeth may be glazed or blunt, or the saw may be underpowered.

To clean the blade, buy a round 12-inch pizza pan and keep it for saw-blade cleaning. Soak the blade in blade-cleaning solution or in oven cleaner. Scrub it clean with a brass-bristled brush or with a Scotch-Brite pad.

Don't try to sharpen a carbide-tipped saw blade yourself. Send it out to be done professionally.

If a clean, new, or newly sharpened, 24-tooth blade still burns, then you may be feeding the wood too slowly. If the saw bogs down when you feed more quickly, then the machine is underpowered for the job.

SAFE RIPPING

Ripping on the table saw requires an auxiliary fence, splitter, and blade guard. The auxiliary fence is a short board screwed onto the manufacturer's rip fence. It should extend from the near end of the fence to the far end of the blade and no farther. If a board should distort during the cut, the short fence won't push it into the blade, thus avoiding kickback.

The splitter, or riving knife, is vital when ripping. It prevents kickback by keeping the wood from pinching the back edge of the saw blade.

The guard should show you where the blade is, protect you from accidentally running your fingers into the blade, and permit you to see the work through it. Badly designed guards are sore spots with many craftsmen.

But your response should be to replace the inadequate guard with a better aftermarket version, not to discard it entirely.

When ripping on the table saw, stand to the left where you can see the blade and keep an eye on the contact between the wood and the fence. Push the work past the blade, but never reach over the top of the blade.

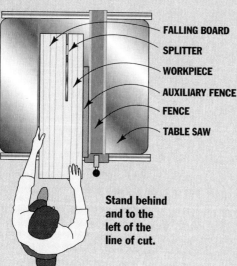

FALLING BOARD

SPLITTER

WORKPIECE

AUXILIARY FENCE

FENCE

TABLE SAW

Stand behind and to the left of the line of cut.

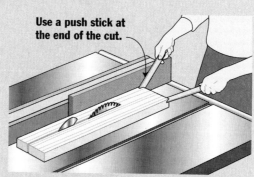

Use a push stick at the end of the cut.

- Focus on contact between the fence and the workpiece.
- Don't overreach.
- Always use a splitter.
- Keep plenty of push sticks on hand.

Safe ripping on the table saw depends upon correctly using all of the equipment: splitter, short auxiliary fence, and blade guard. For clarity, the blade guard is not shown in these illustrations.

You can also rip to width on the band saw if you prefer. If your band saw leads to one side or the other, you'll find it more accurate to snap a chalkline on the wood and to guide the wood through the saw by eye. Keep to the waste side of the line. You'll have to clean up the band-sawn edge by hand planing or machine jointing.

Planing to Thickness

The thickness planer is unique among woodworking machines in that it has only one function. It's also among the safest machines, as long as you don't reach inside while it's on. The only rule to observe is to plane with the grain of your workpiece; otherwise, you'll get chip out. When planing many parts that are destined to be the same final thickness, plane them all at the thickness setting before adjusting the machine for the next cut.

The small portable thickness planers that have appeared on the market in recent years are generally very good. Their most common problem is the tendency to snipe—produce a deep gouge across the end of a board. Sniping occurs when the infeed roll lets go of the board, allowing the last few inches to bounce into the cutterhead. You may be able to minimize snipe if you build an outfeed support table for your machine or if you press the board up or down for the last 12 inches of the cut, as shown in *Preventing Snipe*. If you experiment a little with some scrap, you'll soon discover how to minimize or eliminate snipe on your machine.

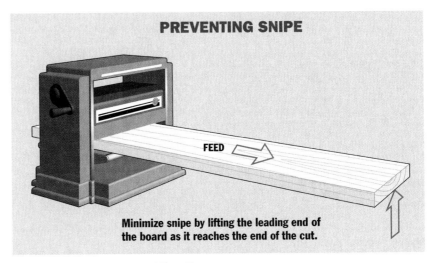

PREVENTING SNIPE

FEED

Minimize snipe by lifting the leading end of the board as it reaches the end of the cut.

Squaring an End

Saw one end of the piece square to the face side and edge. You can do it with a table saw, a chop saw, a radial-arm saw, or hand tools. Regardless of which machine you use, put the face side of the wood down on the machine table and the face edge against your crosscut guide. Use your combination square to verify that the guide is exactly at 90 degrees.

If you're working by hand, knife a line around the workpiece, always registering your square against the face side or the face edge. Saw to the outside of the line, then stand the piece upright in a vise and plane the end to the knifed line. Avoid splitting

FACT OR FICTION

PLANING END GRAIN

Contrary to folklore, a block plane is not the best tool for planing end grain. On wide boards, use a jointer plane because of its heft and because it's big enough to be controlled with great accuracy. Hold the plane slightly askew so it shears the ends of the wood fibers.

at the end of the cut by planing from both directions; with smaller pieces, use scrap wood to back up the workpiece as you plane.

Sawing the Other End Square and to Length

When cutting the last end of the workpiece, shoot for the precise length you want on the first cut. Don't sneak up to the length with several passes.

Use a chop saw or a table saw with a sliding crosscut table. Put your workpiece in position, then bring a stop block up to the end you previously squared. Clamp the stop block in position and make the cut. Using a stop block makes cutting multiples easy, and it gives you a point of reference if you have to recut a piece that is a bit too long.

Note: Each cut throws sawdust against the fence and stop block that can interfere with the accuracy of subsequent crosscuts. Clear the chips after every cut. Also, rabbeting the end of the stop block will create a place for stray chips.

Problem Solving
Crosscutting on the Table Saw

The ability to make a square crosscut at an accurate length is absolutely crucial to joinery. If your cut is wrong when you are preparing the wood, it will still be wrong when you want to saw square shoulders for your joints.

PROBLEM	SOLUTION
There's a saw mark or a groove near the middle of the end grain.	The blade may be wobbling on the saw arbor, or it may be blunt. Sharpen it, and if the problem persists, check the bearings of your saw's arbor to locate and correct the problem.
The end grain is rough.	Invest in a good carbide-tipped saw blade, which will cost about $100. A 40-tooth blade is fine enough; a blade with more teeth won't necessarily make a smoother cut. The alternate-top-bevel configuration is best for crosscutting.
The crosscut is not square to the surface of the board.	Check the blade-tilting mechanism. There may be a pack of sawdust preventing it from coming up to square.
My crosscuts vary: some are square, some are more than 90 degrees, and some are less.	Check the fit of your miter gauge in the table slots and the tightness of the gauge on its bar. If there's a problem, don't wrestle with poor equipment. Instead, make yourself a sliding crosscut box, as shown.

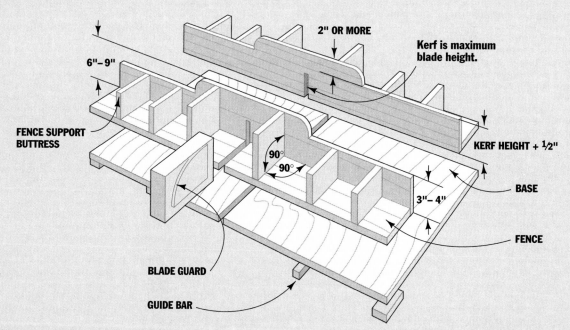

Unless your table saw has a sliding table, a good sliding crosscut box is essential. This is one fixture that's worth the trouble to make well. Rather than making a universal box, which would be big and unwieldy, make two: one for boards 12 inches wide and less and one for wide panels.

Sharpening Tools

Many amateur craftsmen avoid hand tools, even though it's clear that the best way to work wood is to use hand tools along with machines. One reason people avoid hand tools is because they are blunt, and blunt tools don't work for anyone. Once a chisel or plane iron is ground, sharpening it should take about 30 seconds and no longer than 90 seconds. Here is some advice to help you acquire the knack of sharpening:

- A chisel or a plane iron has a grinding angle of 25 degrees and a sharpening angle between 30 and 40 degrees. Grind to a low angle on an electric wheel equipped with a soft, fast-cutting stone (60- to 120-grit), then sharpen the edge of the ground bevel on a flat stone.

- Always grind with the aid of a tool rest. To avoid burning the steel, don't grind right to the edge of the iron. When you've got a nicked iron, put it straight into the wheel to grind past the damage, then grind the bevel as a separate step.

- There's nothing wrong with traditional oilstones, but I prefer waterstones. They cut more quickly, they're easier to maintain, and I think they give a better result. Buy an 800- and a 1,200-grit red stone and the largest 4,000-grit gray stone you can afford. Store your waterstones in a bucket of water, but keep it from freezing.

- The sharpening motion, and the ability to maintain a consistent angle, comes from the shoulders, not from the elbows. You have to get right on top of the sharpening stone, as shown in the photos.

- Before you sharpen any new chisel or plane iron, flatten its back on the 800-grit red stone. The back of the blade is one side of the sharp edge, and it has to be flat and mirror smooth. This step has to be done only once in the life of the tool. Lay the working end of the blade flat on the stone, and press down as hard as you can while you work it back and forth. The objective is to extend the new flat zone to the entire width of the cutting edge. Then polish the back of the blade on your finer stones.

- There is no "correct" sharpening angle. The bevel has to be flat, and the angle should be consistent, but it can vary from 30 to 40 degrees, depending on what you are cutting. Harder wood requires a higher angle.

- The basic sharpening technique consists of three moves: Hone the bevel on a 1,200-grit red stone until you raise a burr on the back of the blade. Move to a fine gray stone and polish the bevel. Finally, flip the blade over and polish the back, also on the gray stone, until you remove the burr.

- To check your sharpening angle, cut a 35-degree angle on the end of a scrap. Rest the blade on the block, feel the angle, remove the block, and then maintain the angle as you work the blade on the stone. Sharpen in a straight line, not in a circular motion or a figure eight. It

may seem easier to sharpen with the edge of the blade parallel to the long edge of the stone, instead of at right angles, but the edge will be fragile, and it will get dull more quickly.

- On a waterstone, if you get the sharpening angle wrong, you're liable to gouge the stone, and you'll have to rub it flat again. To avoid digging into the stone, shift your grip closer to the edge of the chisel or plane iron, and try to use a little less pressure. Separate pressure from control, and work on control before you increase the pressure.

The typical workbench is too high for sharpening, so I made this special workstation. The height is level with my fingertips when I stand straight with my arms at my side. Bench height is the secret of sharpening, since it allows you to get on top of the tool as you hone it. Hold the blade in both hands (inset), and move it over the stone by rocking your entire body back and forth to maintain the angle.

3

EDGE-TO-EDGE JOINTS: MAKING BOARDS WIDER

Key Ingredients

When you need wood that's wider than what came off of the tree, you'll have to join it in width—a process known as edge joining. Because the wood fibers are all basically parallel, and you're gluing one long-grain surface to another long-grain surface, you aren't going to introduce a conflict due to wood movement, as shown in *Wood Movement in Panels*. Thus, once you've glued together a number of boards, you can treat the resulting panel as one large board.

These two panels were glued up from a number of narrow pieces. The pieces were cut from wider boards to take advantage of different grain patterns—cathedral in the upper panel and quarter-sawn in the bottom one.

FACT OR FICTION

SHOULD YOU ROUGH UP THE GLUING SURFACE?

Many people think that a roughened surface will make the best glue joint. They imagine the glue soaks into the wood's crevices and splinters and holds on mechanically like a million little dowels. This is mechanical adhesion, and it does occur, but the resulting matrix of wood and thickened glue is not strong. A damaged surface cannot form a strong glue bond.

A strong bond results when a very thin layer of glue separates two smooth surfaces. The strength results from polar attraction between the wood cells and glue molecules, a phenomenon called specific adhesion.

Glue sticks best to wood that has been cut cleanly and freshly. The smoother the wood, the better the joint. Don't do anything to roughen the surfaces.

Modern glue is stronger than wood. When the joint is broken, the wood breaks on either side of the glue line.

Glue Is All You Need

Because modern glues are stronger than the wood itself, glue alone is all you need to make edge joints. You can easily test this for yourself by making a sample joint, then breaking it along the glue line. You'll find that the wood breaks on one side or the other of the glue line, as shown in the photo (above). This means there is no need to strengthen the joint with splines, tongues, or biscuits. All of these devices are use-

WOOD MOVEMENT IN PANELS

Boards joined in width will move across the grain, but they'll behave as one board.

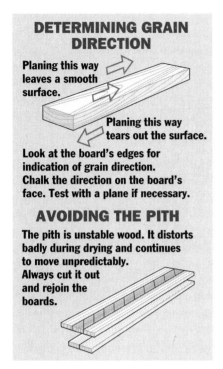

DETERMINING GRAIN DIRECTION

Planing this way leaves a smooth surface.

Planing this way tears out the surface.

Look at the board's edges for indication of grain direction. Chalk the direction on the board's face. Test with a plane if necessary.

AVOIDING THE PITH

The pith is unstable wood. It distorts badly during drying and continues to move unpredictably. Always cut it out and rejoin the boards.

ful for keeping the wood aligned while the glue sets up, but they don't make the joint stronger.

Aesthetic vs. Technical Considerations

In edge-to-edge glue-ups, technical considerations generally are secondary to appearance, but they are worth considering. These include moisture content, grain direction, and the presence of the pith and other abnormal wood. The importance of moisture content is discussed on pages 6–7 and 23; what you do about the grain direction and the pith follows.

Determine grain direction. You'll get the best-looking results if you can hand plane the entire surface of the glued panel. To do this, the grain must run in the same direction on either side of a glue line. Otherwise, it will tear out no matter which way you plane.

To orient the grain in the same direction, look closely at the edge of

each board, and see if you can detect whether the fibers are running upward to the left, upward to the right, or dead level. If you aren't sure, plane a few shavings and find out. Mark the grain direction with a chalk arrow on the board's surface, as shown in *Determining Grain Direction.*

Once you have the glue-up arranged the way you want it (for more on this, see "Choosing Your Boards" on page 22), see whether you can turn some boards end for end, so the grain runs out of the surface in the same direction on both sides of each glue line. Most times, you'll be able to arrange a good compromise. Appearance remains paramount, though, and I won't sacrifice it for ease of cleaning up the panel after glue-up, even if I have to sand.

Note that if the tree grew with a pronounced curve in its trunk, as cherry is prone to do, the wood fibers may run out of the surface in both directions. You'll still find it helpful to locate the point where the fibers change direction because when hand planing, you'll have to change direction to suit the wood.

Rip the heart out. You'll want to rip boards that contain the pith, or heart, of the tree to separate the pith from the usable wood on either side. This is because the pith is liable to move in unpredictable ways—it

RIPPINGS

HOW WIDE TO GLUE UP?

When you glue up your panel, you'll find it much easier to set and adjust the clamps if you don't also have to fool around with glue blocks to protect the edge of your panel from the clamps. Therefore, don't skimp on width when you select the wood. Make the panel an inch wider than its final dimensions. Then after the glue has set, you can saw the panel true and square—and saw off any clamp dings in the process.

probably will cause the board to cup, and the board will likely crack as well. You'll avoid problems by edge gluing two narrow boards, minus the pith, as shown in *Avoiding the Pith.*

Triangles Record Your Decisions

Once you have the boards arranged the way you want them, chalk a triangle onto the surface, as shown in *Marking Your Arrangement.* There's only one way to reassemble the triangle, so you can move the boards around without losing track of your arrangement. Use chalk instead of pencil or crayon so you can brush or wash it off if you change your mind.

MARKING YOUR ARRANGEMENT

When you've decided how to arrange the wood, chalk a triangle on the surface so you can keep the boards in order.

Choosing Your Boards

When you edge glue, you're generally making carcase tops and sides, door panels, or tabletops. These pieces are the show wood—the part of your furniture that everybody sees. Therefore, you'll want to select the best-looking wood you have and arrange its figure in the most pleasing way. This is a design detail you can afford to indulge in because all it costs you is your time.

As you're sorting through your stock, keep in mind that there are reasons to rip some of the pieces apart before gluing them together, as well as reasons to choose one sort of grain over another. Some guidance in these matters follows.

Ripping Wide Boards

Everybody likes a nice, wide plank. Beginning woodworkers often think it sacrilegious to rip wide planks into narrow pieces, then glue them back together again. But you often do exactly that to get the look you want and also to get the most out of your wood.

As you can see in *Getting the Most from Wide Boards*, a wide plain-sawn board always includes some wood that's rift-sawn, almost quarter-sawn, at its edges and some wood that's flat-sawn in its center. This means the figure near the edges will be quite straight, while the center figure will show long vees, known as cathedral figure.

My preference is to rip the straight-grained, quarter-sawn wood from the edges of wide boards (especially oak because of its pronounced rays). I make wide, stable panels from these straight-grained pieces, as shown in the photo on page 20 (bottom), leaving the flat-sawn cathedral figure for narrow rails and stiles. This is simply a personal preference—it makes as much sense to use the cathedral pieces for the wide panel and to reserve the quartered rippings for rails and stiles. Whatever your preference, the point is to select the wood with care and to take maximum advantage of the design possibilities in your material.

The limitations of your equipment may also force you to rip wide boards. You can't flatten the face of a 12-inch plank on an 8-inch jointer. But you can rip it into two 6-inch boards or three 4-inch boards, joint them, and then glue them back together. In this situation, you'll probably be the only one who can even find the glue line. See "Safe Ripping" on page 16 for some table saw techniques.

Quarter-Sawn vs. Flat-Sawn Wood

When you need the flattest and most stable result, you should choose quarter-sawn wood. Quarter-sawn wood is usually expensive and sometimes hard to get, but it is the least liable to warp and twist. When the humidity changes, it's also going to move less in width than flat-sawn wood. The trade-off is that there will be more movement in thickness, but this is generally inconsequential.

Except in species with pronounced rays, such as white oak, quartered wood has the plainest, straightest figure—you generally trade showiness for stability. Along with it, you sometimes get exquisite subtlety—a bonus—courtesy of the ray cells. In cherry, these cells can show as a cluster of little iridescent squares, as shown in the photo. It's also surprising how often you get curly grain on the quarter. Nevertheless, in most hardwoods, the rays' primary effect is to soften the figure, to overlay a shimmering haze across the straight lines of the annual rings.

Most of the time, however, you'll be working with the cathedral figure of flat-sawn wood. Flat-sawn wood tends to cup as the atmospheric humidity changes. The

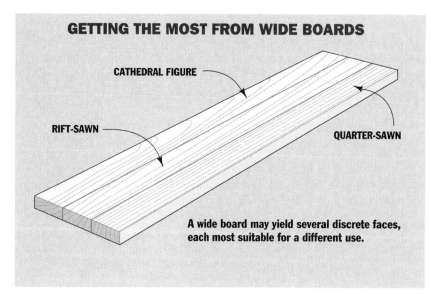

GETTING THE MOST FROM WIDE BOARDS

CATHEDRAL FIGURE

RIFT-SAWN

QUARTER-SAWN

A wide board may yield several discrete faces, each most suitable for a different use.

amount of cupping depends on the change in moisture conditions. You can minimize cupping by storing your wood indoors before you begin to work it. Bringing wood from outdoor storage into conditioned space for just a few weeks will make all the difference.

If the change in moisture conditions is so great that cupping may be a problem, how can you predict which way the board will go? Look at the end grain. By doing so, you can see where the board was relative to the center of the tree. Flat-sawn wood tends to cup toward the bark side as it loses moisture, as shown in *How Flat-Sawn Boards Tend to Cup.*

Ray fleck is the cross-section of ray cells that radiate outward from the heart of the tree. In quarter-sawn cherry, ray fleck is subtly beautiful.

Coping with Cupping

If you pay attention to moisture conditions, cupping becomes a very minor problem in most instances. But what if you are working in a dry shop in winter, and your region has humid summers? What if you are

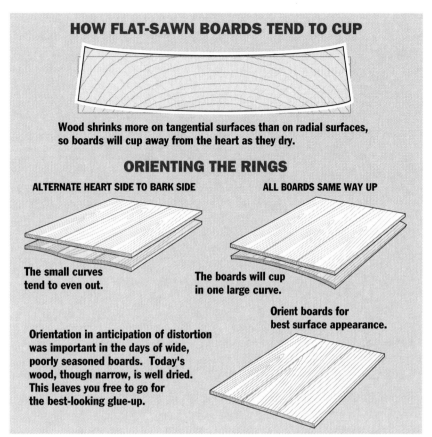

HOW FLAT-SAWN BOARDS TEND TO CUP

Wood shrinks more on tangential surfaces than on radial surfaces, so boards will cup away from the heart as they dry.

ORIENTING THE RINGS

ALTERNATE HEART SIDE TO BARK SIDE

The small curves tend to even out.

ALL BOARDS SAME WAY UP

The boards will cup in one large curve.

Orient boards for best surface appearance.

Orientation in anticipation of distortion was important in the days of wide, poorly seasoned boards. Today's wood, though narrow, is well dried. This leaves you free to go for the best-looking glue-up.

working in rainy Seattle on a piece for your sister in Phoenix? If you anticipate moisture trouble, which way should you arrange the boards? You have three choices, as shown in *Orienting the Rings.* Which one is best depends upon the construction of your piece, for that can play a large role in restraining (or avoiding) distortion. Here are some things to consider:

- In terms of construction, keep the boards or panels narrow. Many designs can be modified to use two or more narrow pieces in place of a wide one.
- Alternate the boards heart side to bark side. The inevitable cupping will tend to even out, showing up as small ripples in the surface. This approach is best for unsupported tops, such as table leaves.

- Arrange all boards the same way up. This way, the whole panel is likely to cup in one large curve, like a potato chip. You will be able to hold the panel flat with screws or wooden buttons screwed into the supporting structure or with a breadboard end. This approach is best for leg-and-apron constructions such as tables, where the top is supported by a rigid framework.

Since I always go for the best-looking panel, I can't give priority to a specific arrangement. Instead, I minimize cupping by paying attention to moisture content. In unusual moisture conditions, I'll control any distortion by restraining the glue-up, for example by using frame-and-panel constructions.

Jointing Edges for Glue-Up

To make a perfect edge joint, all you need is glue—plus two perfectly square, straight, and clean mating edges. You can get an excellent result straight from the jointer, provided your cutters are sharp and that you know what to do. Follow these steps:

STEP 1 Set up your jointer for a light cut, and use a machinist's square to set the fence as square to the table as you can.

STEP 2 Mark the face side of the boards you want to join.

STEP 3 Joint one long edge of each board.

STEP 4 Stand one board on edge in the vise, jointed edge up, and set the other jointed edge on top of it. Keep the face side of both boards toward you.

Hold your straightedge across the joint on the face side, as shown in *Checking the Joint*. The surfaces should line up with no deviation from flatness.

STEP 5 If the faces don't line up, adjust your fence and try again.

RIPPINGS

THE PERFECT EDGE
To produce the cleanest glue surfaces, many woodworkers use a power jointer to remove wood and establish basic flatness, straightness, and squareness. Then they cut off the rippled machine marks with a long jointer plane.

Note: Some books advocate jointing alternate faces against the fence to cancel any error of squareness. However, this means you give up your carefully prepared face side. I prefer to adjust the jointer fence until it cuts square.

Jointing on the Table Saw

It's possible to glue up straight from the table saw, and for many utility constructions, the fit and finish will be entirely adequate. The quality of the sawn edge depends a lot upon the condition of the edge that rides against the rip fence. If this "off-side" edge isn't reasonably straight, the edge you saw won't be straight either. You will get the best results from a sharp carbide-tipped saw blade; my preference is either an alternate-top-bevel (ATB) blade with between 45 and 65 teeth or a hollow-ground steel planer blade. Saw in the following sequence:

STEP 1 Rip the off-side edge straight. Always cut so there is a bit of falling wood, as shown in the photo. Otherwise, the unbalanced forces will shove the cut out of square.

STEP 2 Put the newly sawn edge against the fence and cut the "good" edge, leaving a trace of falling wood as before, and your joint line will be quite good.

STEP 3 Return to the first edge and cut it again. This extra step eliminates inaccuracies resulting from an out-of-square off-side edge and yields the best possible result.

Always rip so there is falling wood. If you kiss the wood with the saw blade, the cut won't be square. To rip safely, stand out of the kickback path, press the wood down on the table and against the fence with your left hand, and move it forward with your right hand.

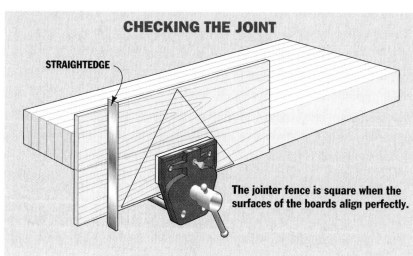

CHECKING THE JOINT

STRAIGHTEDGE

The jointer fence is square when the surfaces of the boards align perfectly.

Jointing with Hand Tools

You can make a perfect edge joint with a long jointer plane. The theory is simple: Just make the edges perfectly square and perfectly straight. You'll get the best results from a 20- or 22-inch jointer plane—a Record or Stanley No. 06 or No. 07. The long sole bridges hollows and hills, bringing them down to level. The iron of the jointer plane must be sharpened dead straight and square, with no curvature.

Hand Planing Square Edges

Good technique with the jointer plane begins with a good stance: feet apart and shoulders loose. The motion comes from your legs, back, and hips, not from your arms, as follows:

STEP 1 Fold each mating pair of edges so the face sides are together, and stand them on the bench or clamp them in a vise with the edges aligned, as shown in *Hand Planing an Edge Joint.*

STEP 2 Take a single thin shaving off the edge of both boards, from one end to the other. By planing both edges at once, any variation from squareness cancels when you butt the edges together.

If the boards are narrow, plane the long edges on the bench top against an end stop; if the boards are wide, put them in a vise and then plane. Planing on the bench top gives you instant feedback: If you aren't planing square and straight, the boards will fall over.

STEP 3 Check the edge for squareness with a try square and for straightness by sighting the board from end to end, as if you were aiming a rifle. Mark high spots and hills with chalk.

STEP 4 Plane again, keeping the wood centered under the iron. Aim toward taking a single long shaving from end to end. Check your progress by eye and with a square.

You may think it difficult to plane straight and square, but your body already knows all about vertical and level; otherwise, you would not be able to stand upright. You can learn how to sense vertical and level with a tool in your hand. First try it by holding the plane (or any other tool) in the air. Close your eyes and tilt the tool. Bring it back to what feels like level and flat, then open your eyes and check. Trust the clues your muscles send you.

Testing the Fit

Test fit each joint by clamping one board in a vise and standing the other board on top of it. The surfaces of the boards should be aligned when you lay a straightedge across the joint, and there should be no rocking.

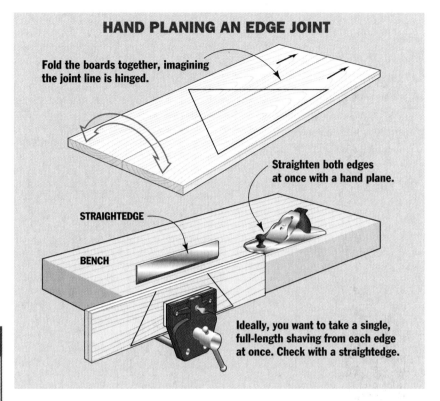

HAND PLANING AN EDGE JOINT

Fold the boards together, imagining the joint line is hinged.

Straighten both edges at once with a hand plane.

STRAIGHTEDGE

BENCH

Ideally, you want to take a single, full-length shaving from each edge at once. Check with a straightedge.

Gluing Up a Panel

All of your preparation will be wasted if your glue-up becomes frantic and goes badly. Glue can set quickly, and there is no going back, except to re-rip and start over. Gluing up should be a relaxed and orderly procedure.

Begin by clamping the whole assembly dry. This way you can check the alignment and the placement of clamps, and you can fetch everything you will need.

Spreading the Glue

Some people brush on glue, some use a small, short-nap paint roller, and others resort to using their fingers. With most edge joints, I find it quickest and easiest to use the wood itself to spread the glue, as shown in "Gluing an Edge Joint."

Clamping Edge-Glued Panels

Lay a minimum of three clamps across the gluing table, and ease the assembly down onto them. Then fill in between with clamps on top of the panel. When you first close the joints, the glue will float the wood, and the edges will swim out of alignment. You can ensure alignment with splines or biscuits, which are discussed in "Keeping the Glue-Up in Line" on page 28. What I usually do is simpler. I snug up the clamps until the glue grabs and begins to squeeze out of the joint. At this point, the wood will stop floating, and the joint will stay put. Then I ease off the clamps a bit, just enough to allow me to realign the joints and position and

tighten the clamps where I want them to be.

Tuning the Squeeze

You can adjust the glue-up by the way you place and adjust your clamps, as shown in *Fine-Tuning a Glue-Up*. Here are the steps:

STEP 1 Snug the center clamp, pushing any errant boards into line.

Make sure the clamp is square across the assembly, or else it will pull the boards lengthwise, out of alignment.

STEP 2 Proceed to the ends of the panel, alternating clamps over and under the work and keeping them square and centered. Tease misaligned boards into line as you do.

STEP 3 Use your straightedge to check for flatness. You can fine-tune flatness by tightening the clamps on one side of the panel more than the ones on the other and by shifting some clamps so their axis of pressure is off the center of the stock. In some situations, you may need to add a clamp or two to one side of the assembly.

If nothing seems to help, the edges may not be square. In this case, you'll have to scrape the glue off of the edges and rejoint them.

Note that oak and other woods containing tannic acid will stain black wherever wet glue comes into contact with steel clamps; a layer of waxed paper will prevent this chemical reaction.

How Tight to Clamp

With most modern glues, you will have between 5 and 10 minutes to fiddle, which is just about enough time. When everything is

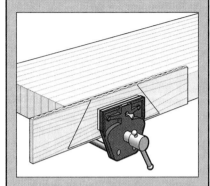

STEP 1 Put a board on edge in a vise and apply a bead of glue to the edge.

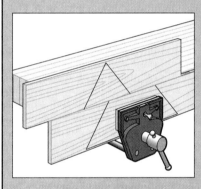

STEP 2 Butt your second board on top of the first, and work it back and forth over a 6-inch sweep, with a little side play.

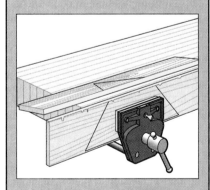

STEP 3 Break the joint, check the surface to make sure glue coverage is uniform, and then clamp.

FINE-TUNING A GLUE-UP

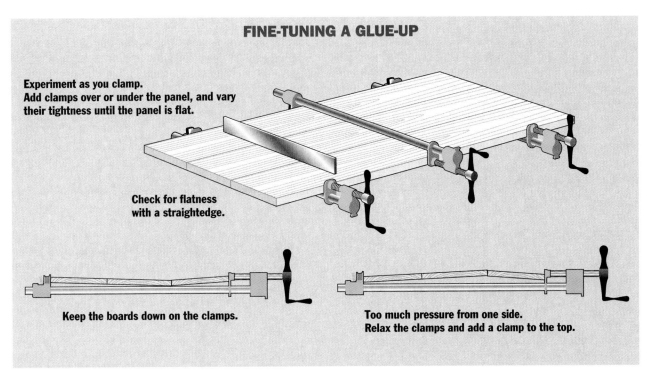

Experiment as you clamp.
Add clamps over or under the panel, and vary their tightness until the panel is flat.

Check for flatness with a straightedge.

Keep the boards down on the clamps.

Too much pressure from one side.
Relax the clamps and add a clamp to the top.

as right as you can make it, tighten the clamps so glue squeezes out all along the joint lines. Do not honk down as hard as you can—if you squeeze too hard, you might drive too much glue out of the joint and starve it.

Firmly hand tight is tight enough; *How Many Clamps* shows why.

If you spread the glue by rubbing the joint, what squeezes out will bead up on the glue line. If you spread the glue on both of the surfaces, however, it will

probably drip and run down the sides of the boards and all over the workpiece as well as all over the bench top. What you want is a small bead of squeeze-out—no more. Every drool is a mess to clean up.

Cleaning Up

What about the glue that squeezed out onto the workpiece? Some craftsmen wash and scrub the squeeze-out off of the panel before they leave the assembly to dry, some lift it off with a chisel after it has partly set up, and others scrape it off after it has set overnight.

Scrubbing off the glue squeeze-out can leave a residue that interferes with finishing. Lifting it off with a chisel might require you to put in a midnight appearance. Although scraping off squeeze-out can tear up the wood, I usually take my chances and scrape in the morning with a heavy-duty paint scraper.

HOW MANY CLAMPS

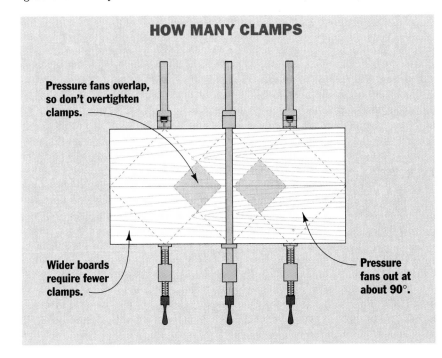

Pressure fans overlap, so don't overtighten clamps.

Wider boards require fewer clamps.

Pressure fans out at about 90°.

Keeping the Glue-Up in Line

Many woodworkers prefer to use some mechanical means, such as biscuits or splines, to keep the surfaces flush when joining edges. For most glue-ups, I don't think these are worth the extra work, but for a complex assembly or if the wood tends to be bowed, they can help a lot.

Aligning with Biscuits

Biscuit joinery is quite fast and accurate. It can ensure close alignment at the surface of the joint while permitting a surprising amount of end-to-end movement. A single row of biscuits spaced 8 to 12 inches apart is usually ample.

STEP 1 Lay the assembly in position on the bench top. Locate the biscuits by making tick marks across the joints.

STEP 2 Cut the slots. I usually remove the biscuit joiner's fence and run the machine's sole directly on the bench top, as shown in *Locating Biscuits*. This eliminates error by relying on the fixed distance from sole to cutter—a setting I can't accidentally change.

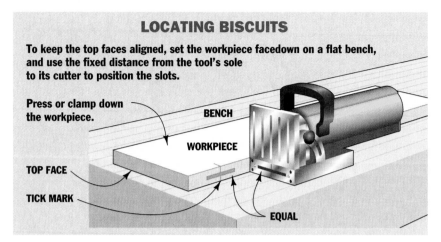

LOCATING BISCUITS

To keep the top faces aligned, set the workpiece facedown on a flat bench, and use the fixed distance from the tool's sole to its cutter to position the slots.

Press or clamp down the workpiece.

BENCH

WORKPIECE

TOP FACE

TICK MARK

EQUAL

If there is any variation in the thickness of your boards, lay them facedown on the bench so their top surfaces are the alignment surfaces.

STEP 3 Once the slots are cut, use a small, stiff brush to work the glue into the voids. I use a ten cent plumber's flux brush with its bristles trimmed to about ¼ inch. Also apply glue to the biscuit. The glue won't transfer from one surface to another well enough by itself.

Aligning with Splines

You also can keep boards in line with a wooden spline that fits in a groove sawn in the adjoining pieces, as shown in *Sizing Splines*. The disadvantage is that splines are trouble to make, and they will show unless you stop the groove at both ends.

Cut the grooves on the table

saw—the width of a regular saw cut is the right thickness for splines. Make the splines from the same stock as your workpieces, and make sure they fit in their grooves, as follows:

STEP 1 Make the spline grooves first. Choose an ATB carbide saw blade because it makes a very clean kerf. Raise the blade so the cut is about ⁵⁄₁₆ inch deep.

STEP 2 Set the table saw's rip fence so the groove is roughly centered on the stock.

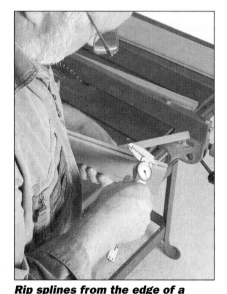

Rip splines from the edge of a board that's as thick as the spline width. I verify the thickness of splines with a dial caliper.

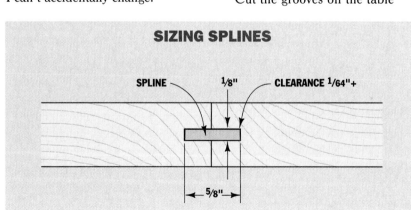

SIZING SPLINES

SPLINE   1/8"   CLEARANCE 1/64"+

5/8"

USING A BISCUIT JOINER

The biscuit joiner has become almost a necessity in today's cabinet shop, and it's a real convenience for home use.

With a biscuit joiner, you can cut matching slots in your workpieces and insert lozenge-shaped hardwood biscuits that register long assemblies or even create joints. The grain of the biscuits, which have been compressed during manufacturing, runs diagonally across the joint line. When the wet glue hits a biscuit, the compressed wood swells and makes a very tight fit.

The sole of the machine has an etched centerline, permitting you to locate a biscuit simply by striking a line across the joint onto both pieces of wood. Bring the machine's centerline up to this line and cut. Here are a few biscuit joiner tips:

- Biscuits come in three standard sizes. Always use the largest that will fit.
- You'll get the most accurate slots if you take the time to clamp the workpiece to your bench.
- Move the machine smoothly and slowly into the workpiece. If you jam it, it will bounce and make a sloppy cut.
- Biscuits can achieve almost perfect alignment in thickness while permitting about ¼ inch of end-to-end movement. This helps you align joints accurately.
- Biscuits are surprisingly strong and can even replace mortise-and-tenon joints in some lighter-duty applications. However, you should double them up whenever possible, in both length and thickness, as shown.

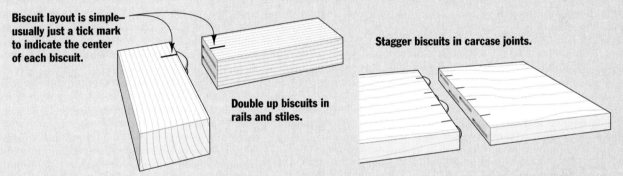

Biscuit layout is simple— usually just a tick mark to indicate the center of each biscuit.

Double up biscuits in rails and stiles.

Stagger biscuits in carcase joints.

Biscuit joinery is a very fast, efficient method of joining wood. Simply strike a centerline across both pieces where you want a biscuit. Then cut matching slots in the pieces by aligning the centerline on the machine with the lines on the work.

STEP **3** With the top face of the wood against the fence, cut the grooves carefully and smoothly.

STEP **4** Measure the depth of the groove and double it. This figure, minus a fat sixty-fourth of clearance, is the spline width. Now measure the width of the groove. This is the spline thickness.

STEP **5** Prepare a board the length of the grooves, and plane it so its thickness equals the spline width.

STEP **6** Rip the splines from the edge of this planed board. If your table saw technique is good, you can rip splines to the precise thickness. Otherwise, rip them oversized, then run them through a planer at a very light setting.

STEP **7** Do a complete dry assembly and clamp it. You may find that the depth of the grooves is inconsistent, which will prevent the joints from closing.

STEP **8** Once you're satisfied with the fit of the splines, spread glue on the edges of the boards and down into the grooves. Then set the splines in place and tap them home.

FACT OR FICTION

ARE DOWELS AN OPTION?

Dowels are not a practical solution to aligning an edge joint. It is difficult to drill precisely matching holes that are all parallel to the face of the wood. Even if you succeed, dowels still can make a good edge joint bad. This is because they introduce a cross-grain element to a long-grain joint. If the wood shrinks too much, the dowels can push the joint apart.

Problem Solving
Making Edge Joints

Making edge joints may seem simple, but there are quite a few things that can go wrong. Here are some solutions to the most common problems.

PROBLEM	SOLUTION
I can't make the jointer plane cut a shaving. It just skids.	Sharpen the iron. A dull plane iron tends to skid without cutting. Even if it does get a start, it's very hard to continue the cut.
The glue set, but the joint had no strength—it broke apart.	The glue line may have been contaminated by dust, oils in the wood, or finishing solvents; or the glue may have been too old. You'll get the best results when you glue up with fresh glue soon after machining or planing the mating edges. Letting the wood hang around for a few weeks invites contamination. Most yellow glues have a shelf life of about one year.
There's a hill in the middle of the board, and I can't seem to plane it away.	Take a very short shaving from the highest point of the hill. Take another shaving a couple of inches longer. Bear down almost entirely on the front knob of the plane, so the newly flat surface guides the cut. As the flat surface gets longer, shift pressure to both the front knob and the handle of the plane.
When I run a test piece over my jointer, I get a square edge, but when I joint my good boards, the edges aren't square.	Your jointer technique is likely to be the problem. Perhaps you're not pressing the face of the stock against the jointer fence, or perhaps the wood bows in its length. When you joint an edge, take care to press the full length of the board against the fence. Thick, heavy planks can deflect the fence of a small jointer, and their mass can fool you into thinking you're working against the fence when in fact, you're simply preserving an out-of-square edge. **Press here.** **To make sure the board stays in close contact with the fence, press hard about 1 inch above the jointer table.**
I made an edge joint using yellow glue, and it turned powdery white overnight.	Could the wood have been colder than 45°F? Cold glue does not set properly; the telltale sign is a white powdery residue. You need a warm shop for gluing up, and wood itself has to warm, which can take hours. For this reason, woodworkers in cold climates generally glue up at the end of the day and leave the shop heated that night.
The glue set before I could align the joints.	Could the wood have been warmer than 80°F? Warm glue sets quickly. In a hot climate, you might have to air-condition the shop or do your gluing during the cool of early morning.

Adding Veneer Inserts

I f you're looking for something a little different, you can use veneer inserts to emphasize a glue line, as shown in the photo. This can do wonders for an otherwise ho-hum panel. You can create a dramatic fine-line effect, with the best results from dyed veneers or woods of strongly contrasting colors, such as maple with walnut. You can decorate a glued-up panel by gluing a slip of veneer into every glue line, if you like, and you can stack as many as three veneers in each glue line. More than three, however, and it would be better to insert solid pieces of wood. Follow these steps for adding veneer inserts:

STEP 1 Use a sharp knife to cut the veneers a scant ¹/₁₆ inch wider than the thickness of the

ELEVATING THE GLUE-UP

¹/₄" × 1" Masonite strips provide clearance for veneer inserts.

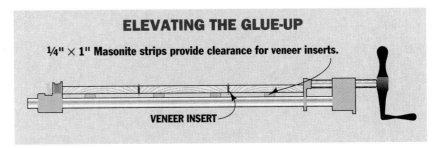

VENEER INSERT

wood. This will give you enough leeway to assemble the panel without interfering with the fundamental alignment of the solid wood.

STEP 2 Apply glue to each side of the veneers and to the boards.

STEP 3 Clamp the assembly together. You can support the boards without interfering with the veneers by laying strips of ¹/₄-inch Masonite across the clamp bars, as shown in *Elevating the Glue-Up*.

If you find it difficult to keep the boards aligned, you can glue up in sections: Glue a pair of boards, with the veneer insert in

between, then assemble the pairs until your panel is complete.

As an alternative, you can also use biscuits to keep a veneered joint aligned, but doing so adds an extra step. Glue the veneer to one side of each joint, using a long, straight piece of wood as a clamping block, as shown in *Gluing the Veneer Separately*. Then clean up the surface, cut the slots in the usual way (see "Aligning with Biscuits" on page 28), and assemble the panel.

Between the veneers and the edges of the boards, there is a lot of surface to cover with glue—and a righteous mess if your glue-spreading technique is not under control. Learn to use a short-nap paint roller, as described in "Gluing Up a Lamination" on page 35. This is the best way to lay down a precise and uniform coating of glue.

GLUING THE VENEER SEPARATELY

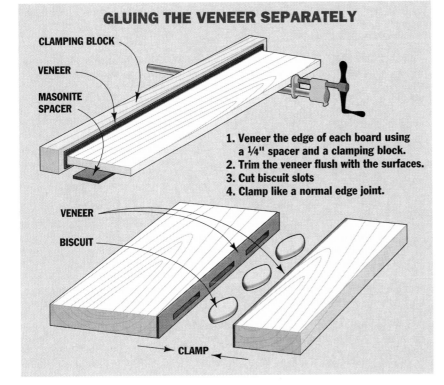

CLAMPING BLOCK
VENEER
MASONITE SPACER

1. Veneer the edge of each board using a ¹/₄" spacer and a clamping block.
2. Trim the veneer flush with the surfaces.
3. Cut biscuit slots
4. Clamp like a normal edge joint.

VENEER
BISCUIT
CLAMP

Veneer inserts make a decorative feature of the glue lines in this tabletop.

PUSHING THE LIMITS: Joinery along Curved Lines

Edge-to-edge joints don't have to be straight lines. You can create interesting effects by cutting matching curves in two pieces of wood, as shown in the photo. One reason for doing this is so you can work with visible shapes in the wood's figure or perhaps to eliminate a large knot; or you may wish simply to create a decorative motif.

An insert of a complementary veneer will emphasize a curved glue line in the same way it will a straight one. (See "Adding Veneer Inserts" on page 31.) In effect, you can draw on the wood with lines of veneer. *A Few Curving Possibilities* suggests some of the effects you can achieve. You're limited only by your imagination.

Band-Sawing the Curves

The easiest way to create the curves is to cut them on the band saw. If you cut both parts of the curve at once, the marks left by the blade will fit together, making a clean glue line when you edge glue the wood together. While a band-sawn edge isn't as good a gluing surface as a clean, smooth one, it is still adequate. Band-sawing the curves is my preferred method if I'm only making a few special panels. Here are the basic steps to get you started:

STEP 1 Prepare the wood so it's a couple of inches longer than the final dimension of the panel you want. This allows you to overlap the boards and screw them together through the waste at the ends. The curves you intend to make will tell you how much extra width you will need at the start. To be sure your boards are big enough, make a full-sized drawing.

STEP 2 Set up the band saw carefully. I prefer a ½-inch, four-tooth-per-inch blade. It is coarse enough to cut quickly, yet narrow enough to follow a gently curved line. Make sure the blade is square to the saw table and properly tensioned. Set the upper guide just above the combined thickness of the two pieces you'll be cutting.

STEP 3 Overlap the boards, as shown in *Preparing for the*

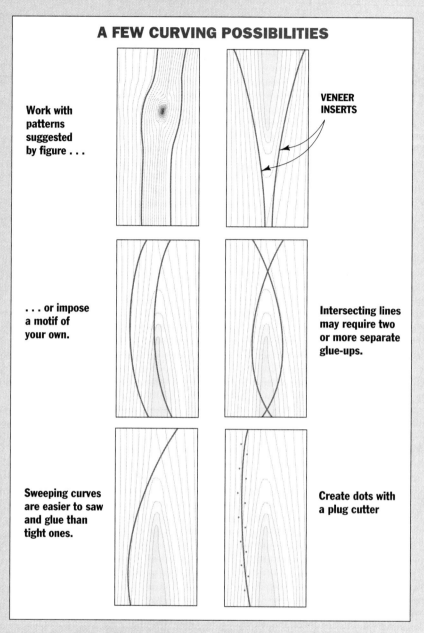

A FEW CURVING POSSIBILITIES

Work with patterns suggested by figure . . .

VENEER INSERTS

. . . or impose a motif of your own.

Intersecting lines may require two or more separate glue-ups.

Sweeping curves are easier to saw and glue than tight ones.

Create dots with a plug cutter

Cut, and draw the cut line on the top surface (or transfer it from your drawing). Gentle, sweeping curves that play off the wood's figure will be easiest to saw and glue up—and are probably the most attractive.

STEP 4 Screw the two boards together through the extra wood at the ends. Make sure the screws aren't in the line of the cut. Also, screw or tape a batten under the unsupported side of the top piece of wood. Make sure the batten will remain on the saw table throughout the cut: If it drops off the edge partway through, the pieces may tip, and you'll have to start over.

STEP 5 Make alignment marks across the pieces, as shown.

STEP 6 Saw the curve. You'll get the best results if you move the wood through the blade without abrupt changes of direction and without stopping and restarting. You might find yourself deviating from your line, but it's better to let the saw go where it will, as long as the result is a smooth, clean curve.

STEP 7 Remove the fasteners and fit the two pieces together.

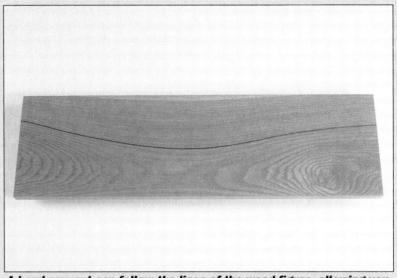

A band saw cut can follow the lines of the wood figure, allowing you to glue up a panel around a knot or other defect.

Now you can glue up just as if the wood were perfectly straight. You can even add a couple of biscuits to help you align the surfaces, though you might have to set the biscuit joiner for a slightly deeper-than-normal cut on the concave side of the curve.

Don't attempt to sand or otherwise refine the band-sawn edges. You won't be able to improve the fit of the sawn surface—you'll only make it less accurate.

If you insert veneers, the marks left by band-sawing will no longer fit together. However, the gaps will be truly tiny, and ordinary yellow glue will fill them. There will be enough long-grain contact to make a strong joint.

You also can cut the curve with an oscillating saber saw or even a scroll saw, if that's the equipment you have. Use the widest blade the saw will accept, which will encourage a gentle, sweeping curve instead of one with a lot of to-and-fro.

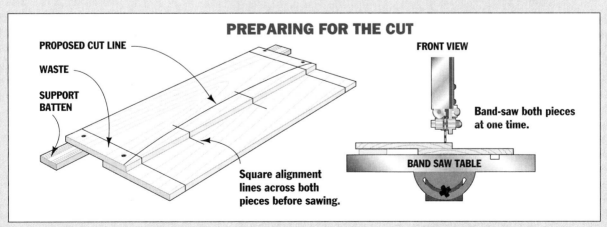

PREPARING FOR THE CUT

PROPOSED CUT LINE

WASTE

SUPPORT BATTEN

Square alignment lines across both pieces before sawing.

FRONT VIEW

Band-saw both pieces at one time.

BAND SAW TABLE

Making Face-to-Face Joints

When you need a leg blank that's 3 inches square in section, you'll often have to glue up the blank from thinner boards. You can do the same thing when you need a massive section, wide and thick, as for a sturdy bench seat, a beam, or the top of a workbench. This is called face lamination, or stack lamination, as shown in *Gluing Up Face to Face*.

A butcher block is a special case of face lamination. The working surface of a true wear-resistant butcher block is end-grain wood. You make it by gluing a long, wide panel, as you would the top of a workbench. Then you crosscut the glue-up into short sections,

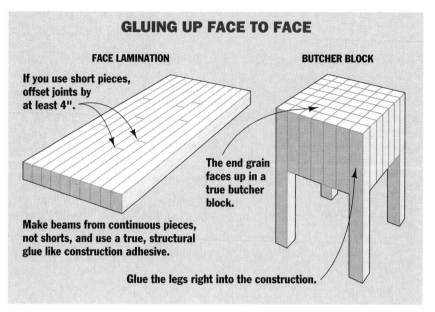

GLUING UP FACE TO FACE

FACE LAMINATION

If you use short pieces, offset joints by at least 4".

Make beams from continuous pieces, not shorts, and use a true, structural glue like construction adhesive.

BUTCHER BLOCK

The end grain faces up in a true butcher block.

Glue the legs right into the construction.

which you glue together face to face to create the block. You can make integral legs by gluing longer pieces into the corners of the assembly.

Butcher blocks and other face

laminations rely on long-grain to long-grain glue joints. As with edge joints, the glue is what holds the wood together, not interlocking parts. So there's no need for biscuits or other reinforcement; however, you may want to add biscuits for help with alignment.

Arranging Boards in a Face-to-Face Joint

If you're face laminating boards to make up a wide plank, you'll end up with the most consistent surface if all of the individual boards were sawn the same way, as shown in *Arranging the Boards*. Aside from appearance, there aren't any real technical considerations. But when gluing up stock for leg blanks, some other factors come into play.

For example, if you need a 3-inch-thick leg blank, there are several ways you might make up that thickness. You could laminate a 8/4 board to one that's 4/4. The single glue line, however, would be subject to a lot of stress if one of the pieces were to move more than the other. You would have a more balanced construction if you used three

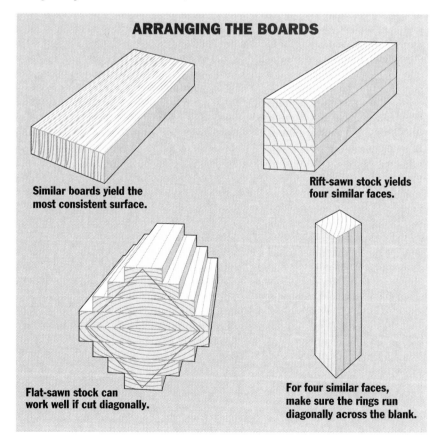

ARRANGING THE BOARDS

Similar boards yield the most consistent surface.

Rift-sawn stock yields four similar faces.

Flat-sawn stock can work well if cut diagonally.

For four similar faces, make sure the rings run diagonally across the blank.

CLAMP FACTS

- A single bar clamp cranked hard can exert about 2,000 pounds of pressure; a pipe clamp can exert somewhat less than that—about 1,500 pounds. Rusted and grimy clamp screws will reduce the squeeze by half.
- Clamping pressure across multiple glue lines is like the voltage in a parallel electrical circuit: Whether one glue line or ten, the pressure is the same across each.
- The right amount of pressure depends somewhat on wood density, but 10 to 15 pounds of pressure per square inch of glue line is minimum, and 200 pounds per square inch is too much. If you want to calculate, use 50 pounds of pressure per square inch as a guide. Thus a single bar clamp can cover 40 square inches of glue line.
- Clamping pressure fans out from the clamp heads, as shown in *How Many Clamps* on page 27. This is why you need a lot of clamps to glue a thin edging to a panel but only a few clamps to edge glue a pair of wide boards. Keep a set of glue blocks handy to help distribute clamping pressure when necessary. Wax them to keep them clean and free of glue dribbles.
- The working faces of bar clamps and C-clamps have to be flat, or the irregularities will misdirect the pressure and dent the work. You'll find the clamps much easier to align if you take the time to file the faces flat and smooth.

pieces of the thinner stock. If one piece moves, the other two probably will keep the glue-up stable. For the most consistent appearance on all four sides of the leg, arrange the rings so they run across the diagonal of the blank, as shown.

Gluing Up a Lamination

You can glue up a face lamination straight from the jointer or planer. As shown in the photo, a roller spreads the glue efficiently.

You don't even have to clean the roller if you intend to use it within a couple of weeks. Simply store it in a resealable plastic bag. Glue doesn't harden in the bottle, and it won't harden in a sealed bag either.

You have to learn by practice how to apply the right amount of glue, but the place to begin is with as little as possible. Roll the glue out evenly on both surfaces, so it just barely wets the wood, with no beads or voids. Be stingy. Not only is glue expensive but excessive squeeze-out also makes a mess.

Clamp the joint together and see how much glue squeezes out. There should be almost none. When you have applied the right amount of glue, it will squeeze out as a row of droplets or beads, not drools or dribbles, along the glue line. Finally, relax the clamps, shove and tap the pieces into alignment, and reclamp tight.

The number of pieces of wood you can clamp at once depends mostly upon the glue's open time, which in turn is a function of temperature. You must have enough time to spread, assemble, clamp, relax, align, and clamp home. In hot weather, you'll be able to do fewer pieces at once than in cooler weather—sometimes just one glue line at a time. In any event, make sure you have everything you need—clamps, clamping blocks, rags, biscuits—before you start spreading glue.

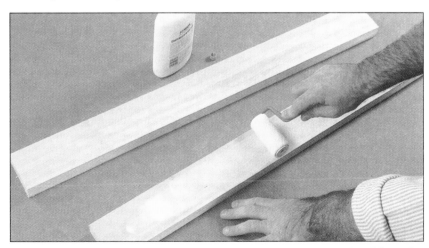

A short-nap 3-inch-wide paint roller is the best way to spread a thin, uniform layer of glue on broad surfaces of wood.

Making Long-Grain Right Angles

You can make the wooden equivalent of angle iron by edge gluing two boards so they form a right angle. Since the joint consists entirely of long-grain glue surfaces, the bond has all the strength you could ever need without additional reinforcement. And since the two pieces of wood are parallel to one another, there is no cross-grain instability to worry about.

There are a surprising number of places where you can use this construction in making furniture, as shown in *Using Wooden "Angle Iron."* A single angle will form an elegant and sturdy table leg. Two together make a square column, again for a table leg or a plant stand. You often see pine cabinets and blanket chests constructed this way.

Gluing a Long-Grain Right Angle

Like any other edge-glued joint, the long-grain right angle must be clamped while the glue sets. It can be difficult to keep the pieces in place, but generally they can be coaxed into line.

Hold one piece in a vise, and apply glue to its edge with a roller. Clamp the second piece in place, as shown in *Clamping a Right Angle.* Tighten the clamps to squeeze out the excess glue, then loosen them, reposition the pieces, and clamp tight to dry. Alternatively, use bar clamps or even nails, as shown.

USING WOODEN "ANGLE IRON"

The body of this plant stand is made from a pair of angles.

Single angles make a blanket chest or cabinet legs.

An inverted angle makes an unusual table leg.

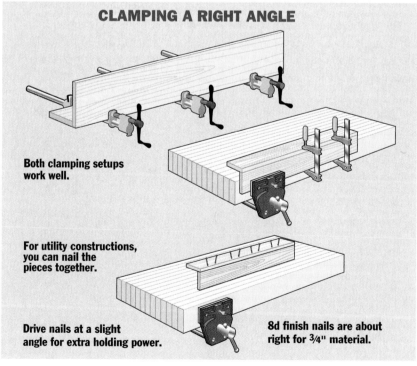

CLAMPING A RIGHT ANGLE

Both clamping setups work well.

For utility constructions, you can nail the pieces together.

Drive nails at a slight angle for extra holding power.

8d finish nails are about right for 3/4" material.

Making a Rabbeted Right-Angle Joint

Rabbeting one-half of a right-angle joint provides alignment in one direction. A rabbet can be made into a very attractive reversed-corner detail if it's sawn short, as shown in *Right-Angle Variations*. The reversed corner can be emphasized with paint or a decorative molding, glued in place after assembly.

Cutting the Rabbet

The table saw offers the safest and quickest way to make a long-grain rabbet. You make two cuts, as shown in *Rabbeting on the Table Saw*. In the first cut, the wood is flat on the table, and in the second, the wood is held vertically against the fence. This arrangement keeps the blade covered for safety, and it ensures that the joint won't be ruined if you bobble the cut.

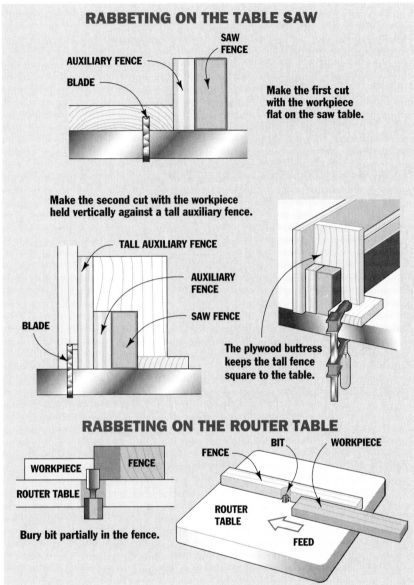

RABBETING ON THE TABLE SAW

SAW FENCE
AUXILIARY FENCE
BLADE

Make the first cut with the workpiece flat on the saw table.

Make the second cut with the workpiece held vertically against a tall auxiliary fence.

TALL AUXILIARY FENCE
AUXILIARY FENCE
BLADE
SAW FENCE

The plywood buttress keeps the tall fence square to the table.

RABBETING ON THE ROUTER TABLE

BIT   WORKPIECE
FENCE
WORKPIECE
FENCE
ROUTER TABLE
ROUTER TABLE
FEED

Bury bit partially in the fence.

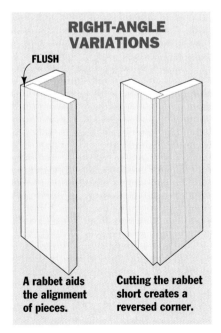

RIGHT-ANGLE VARIATIONS

FLUSH

A rabbet aids the alignment of pieces.

Cutting the rabbet short creates a reversed corner.

The vertical cut should be supported for the full width of the wood, so you need to screw a tall auxiliary fence onto your rip fence, as shown. I usually add a plywood buttress at each end to ensure that the high fence is square and stable.

Routing the Rabbet

You can also cut a long-grain rabbet with a table-mounted router. Hold the wood flat on the table and bury the cutter partially in the fence, as shown in *Rabbeting on the Router Table*. In this setup, you can stay in control of the cut by pressing the wood hard against the table and the fence. If you err and the piece comes off the table or the fence, don't worry—the workpiece won't be ruined. Use a cutter with a diameter about twice the width of the cut. When you rabbet with a large-diameter cutter, the high peripheral velocity permits you to take the full depth at once, so you don't have to waste time nibbling away at it.

Cutting a Rabbet-and-Groove Joint

Y ou can make a wooden right angle using a rabbet-and-groove joint, as shown in *Rabbet-and-Groove Joinery.* The advantage of this joint is that it positively locates both boards. The rabbet creates an off-center tongue. A centered tongue is more difficult to make and fit, and it leaves a more fragile projecting piece toward the outside of the groove.

The groove not only locates the pieces but it also adds gluing area. The groove doesn't have to be big. In fact, I usually make it with a single saw cut to a maximum depth of one-third the thickness of the wood. Cut the groove, then rabbet the second piece to match.

When you clamp, you have to keep clamping pressure over the

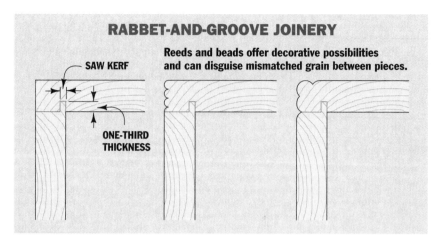

RABBET-AND-GROOVE JOINERY

Reeds and beads offer decorative possibilities and can disguise mismatched grain between pieces.

SAW KERF

ONE-THIRD THICKNESS

joint itself, as shown in *Rabbet-and-Groove Glue-Up.* Otherwise, the joint won't be square.

Making Long-Grain Miters

P robably the cleanest appearing long-grain right-angle joint is the miter. To make it, rip the edges of your boards at 45 degrees, then clean up the sawn edges on the jointer (angle

the fence) or with a large chamfering bit in a table-mounted router.

As with all of the other long-grain edge joints, glue alone is enough to hold a long-grain miter together. The trick is holding the parts in place while the glue sets.

Some woodworkers like to fool around with strap clamps and loose corner blocks, but I don't think such methods work very well. My solution is to rip long, 45-degree clamping blocks and glue them onto the outside of the miter joints, as shown in *Clamping a Miter.*

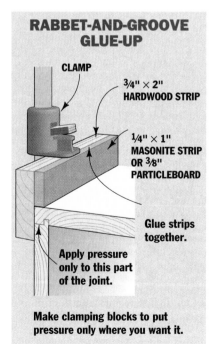

RABBET-AND-GROOVE GLUE-UP

CLAMP

¾" × 2" HARDWOOD STRIP

¼" × 1" MASONITE STRIP OR ⅜" PARTICLEBOARD

Glue strips together.

Apply pressure only to this part of the joint.

Make clamping blocks to put pressure only where you want it.

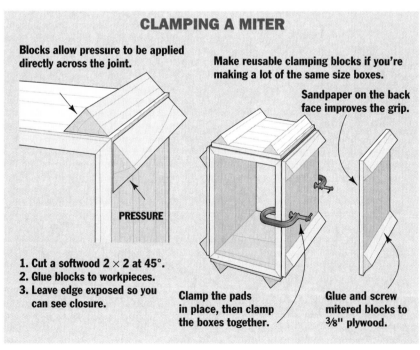

CLAMPING A MITER

Blocks allow pressure to be applied directly across the joint.

PRESSURE

1. Cut a softwood 2 × 2 at 45°.
2. Glue blocks to workpieces.
3. Leave edge exposed so you can see closure.

Make reusable clamping blocks if you're making a lot of the same size boxes.

Sandpaper on the back face improves the grip.

Clamp the pads in place, then clamp the boxes together.

Glue and screw mitered blocks to ⅜" plywood.

Then I put pressure where it's needed with a C-clamp across the blocks. After the glue dries, I saw off the blocks and plane away any residue.

Cutting Splined Miter Joints

Adding a long-grain, solid-wood spline is a good way to keep a long-grain miter joint aligned as you're gluing up. Keep in mind that the spline doesn't make the joint appreciably stronger; in fact, if the spline isn't placed properly, it may actually weaken the joint.

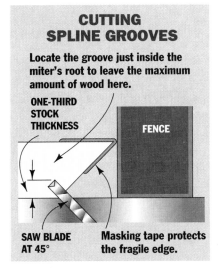

CUTTING SPLINE GROOVES

Locate the groove just inside the miter's root to leave the maximum amount of wood here.

ONE-THIRD STOCK THICKNESS

FENCE

SAW BLADE AT 45°

Masking tape protects the fragile edge.

After you make the miters, cut the groove for the splines on the table saw, as shown in *Cutting Spline Grooves*. Tilt the saw blade to 45 degrees, and run the flat face of the wood on the table, with the point of the miter bearing securely against the fence. You can protect the fragile tip of the miter with a layer of masking tape. Make the width of the groove equal to the thickness of the saw blade, locate it just inside the root of

the miter, and don't go deeper than a third of the way through the wood.

Glue and clamp a splined miter with clamping blocks as you would a regular miter.

Aligning a Miter with Biscuits

Most biscuit joiners come with a 45-degree fence for making slots in the face of miters, as shown in the photo. The geometry of the joint is almost the same as with a splined miter, except the biscuits are intermittent, so there's no risk of weakening the joint. Space the biscuits a hand's breadth apart. The machine's miter fence will govern how far up the face the slots fall. Clamp the same way as you do a splined miter, with triangular blocks glued onto the workpiece.

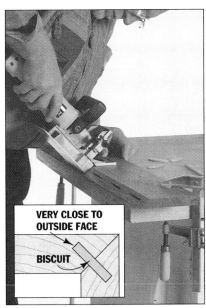

VERY CLOSE TO OUTSIDE FACE

BISCUIT

A biscuit joiner locates a slot away from the root of the miter, a no-no with splined joinery. Here, though, the location is acceptable because the slot is intermittent.

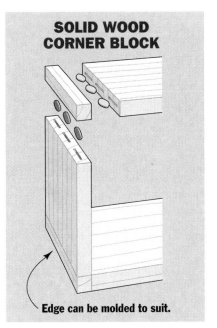

SOLID WOOD CORNER BLOCK

Edge can be molded to suit.

Biscuit-Joining Sheet Goods

The rabbet-and-groove joint, the splined miter, and the miter with biscuits are fundamental joints for building with plywood and medium-density fiberboard (MDF).

In MDF and particleboard, the surface is much denser than the interior mass. When you cut through the surface, as when making grooves, you substantially weaken the sheet. Biscuit joints are better than splines in both plywood and MDF because they leave more of the surface of the material intact.

A solid-wood corner block, joined with biscuits and glue, is also fundamental for working with man-made sheet materials. All that's necessary is to cut the plywood or MDF perfectly straight and square. Space the biscuits about a hand's breadth apart, and be sure to spread glue on the full edge of the plywood. *Solid Wood Corner Block* shows how the joint goes together.

SHOP SOLUTIONS: A Roll-Around Clamp Cart

It's probably possible to have too many clamps, but I have yet to meet a woodworker who's found that limit. The only trouble with having a good-sized collection of clamps is having to store them somewhere while they're not in use. This roll-around clamp cart, designed by Fred Matlack of the Rodale Press Design Shop, is one answer to that problem. It provides ample storage space in a fairly compact unit.

As shown in the photo, the cart will hold a dozen bar clamps, 10 to 20 rapid-action clamps, plus an assortment of hand screws and other, smaller clamps. You can also keep glue, rollers, screws, and other assembly aids on board without worrying about spilling them—the shelves are sloped to keep their contents in place as the cart rumbles along.

The advantage to a roll-around cart is that you can wheel it right over to the action. This may not seem like a big deal, but even in a small shop, carrying more than three or four clamps at once requires more than two hands. If you ever have to do a glue-up that involves every clamp in the shop (like a big bent lamination), you'll be glad you didn't have to lug the clamps around a few at a time. Plus, you won't be as tempted to leave all those clamps in a jumble on the floor after the glue sets.

Build the cart from a decent-quality plywood, like shop-grade birch or even A-C fir. It will look better longer if you take the time to glue ¼-inch strips of hardwood

The ability to move your clamps around the shop all at once is a tremendous time- and back-saver. Add a few small tools like a cordless screw driver and a tack hammer, and you'll have a portable assembly station.

to the visible edges after you cut the pieces to size.

For fast, efficient edging, cut the strips a little wider than necessary (about ⅞ inch for ¾-inch material). Spread glue on the edges, and nail the edging in place with finish nails. When the glue dries, trim the edging flush with a flush-trim bit in a router.

Make the clamp bars from solid wood—something reasonably strong since you will be asking them to support a fair amount of weight. Simply glue and screw the parts of the cart together—

there's no need to get too involved in the joinery.

None of the dimensions are critical. Use those given as a guide, but make the cart to suit your clamp collection as well as the materials you have on hand. As you're doing your planning, you may want to leave a little extra space for future acquisitions.

The one place not to skimp is on the casters—you'll need ones at least 3 inches in diameter to support the cart when it's fully loaded. Clamps are heavy.

EXPLODED VIEW

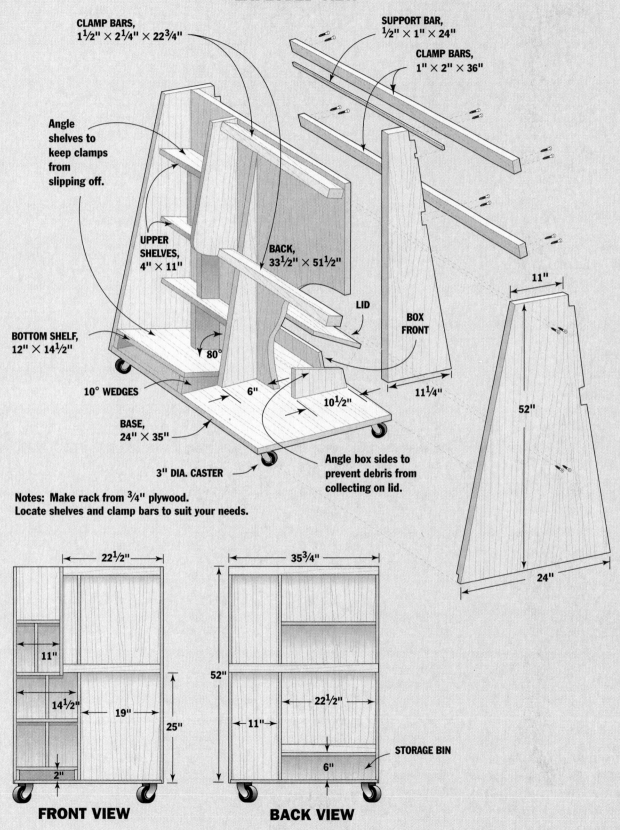

CLAMP BARS,
$1^1/2" \times 2^1/4" \times 22^3/4"$

SUPPORT BAR,
$^1/2" \times 1" \times 24"$

CLAMP BARS,
$1" \times 2" \times 36"$

Angle shelves to keep clamps from slipping off.

UPPER SHELVES,
$4" \times 11"$

BACK,
$33^1/2" \times 51^1/2"$

LID

BOX FRONT

BOTTOM SHELF,
$12" \times 14^1/2"$

80°

$11"$

$52"$

10° WEDGES

$6"$

$10^1/2"$

$11^1/4"$

BASE,
$24" \times 35"$

3" DIA. CASTER

Angle box sides to prevent debris from collecting on lid.

$24"$

Notes: Make rack from $^3/4"$ plywood.
Locate shelves and clamp bars to suit your needs.

$22^1/2"$

$11"$

$14^1/2"$

$19"$

$25"$

$2"$

$35^3/4"$

$52"$

$22^1/2"$

$11"$

STORAGE BIN

$6"$

FRONT VIEW

BACK VIEW

4

RAIL JOINTS: JOINING END GRAIN TO LONG GRAIN

Key Ingredients

The mortise and tenon, with its innumerable variations, is the principal rail joint in woodworking. This joint is the workhorse that holds most furniture together. It's used to make frames for paneled doors and cabinet sides, to connect the elements of complex cabinets, to make the leg-and-apron joint of tables, and to make chairs. *Designing a Mortise-and-Tenon Joint* isolates many of the typical situations where a mortise and tenon is called for and introduces some of the design variations.

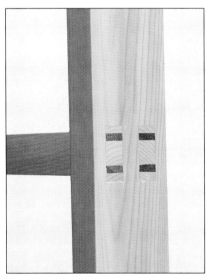

The through wedged mortise and tenon not only makes a very strong connection but also makes a declaration of craftsmanship.

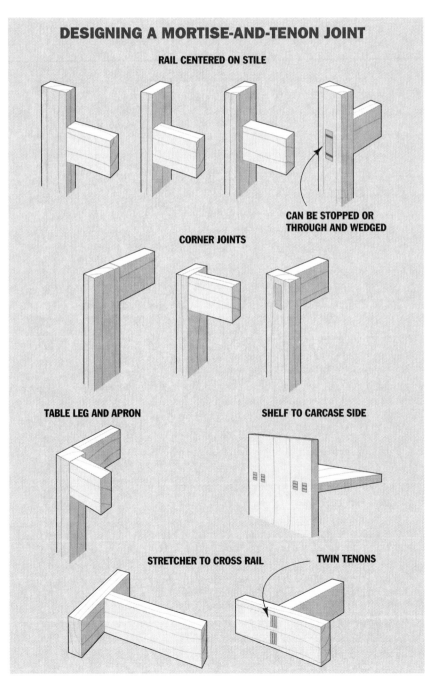

DESIGNING A MORTISE-AND-TENON JOINT

RAIL CENTERED ON STILE

CAN BE STOPPED OR THROUGH AND WEDGED

CORNER JOINTS

TABLE LEG AND APRON

SHELF TO CARCASE SIDE

STRETCHER TO CROSS RAIL

TWIN TENONS

You can make a mortise-and-tenon joint by machine or by hand. In nearly all applications, a single project contains a minimum of four joints and often more. Therefore, it's worthwhile to build jigs and fixtures and to develop sound machine techniques for cutting these joints. But even in highly mechanized shops, it's often easier and faster to cut unusual and unique joints by hand.

Defining Terms

The tenon, or peg, is the male part of the joint; the mortise, or hole, is the female part. *The Anatomy of a Mortise-and-Tenon Joint* shows the parts of the joint, the names of which are also derived from human physiology. Further explanation follows.

- The opening of the mortise is called the mouth. The interior faces, as well as the wood alongside the mortise, are called the cheeks.
- The broad, flat sides of the tenon are called the faces. The wide, flat plane at the base of the tenon is called the shoulder; the narrow part of the shoulder at the edge of the tenon, which doesn't contribute to the strength of the joint, is called the cosmetic shoulder. Once the joint is assembled, the shoulder lines are all you see, so the accuracy with which you lay out and cut the shoulders is critical for visual success.

You can make the joint without one or both of the tenon shoulders (thus forming a bare-faced tenon), but except for such special purposes as fence posts and rails, you shouldn't. Such a joint has little or no stability and is not suitable for furniture.

- The horizontal pieces of a frame, usually with tenons on their ends, are the rails. The vertical pieces, usually mortised, are the stiles.
- When making a mortise near the end of a piece of stock, it's best to add a piece called a horn. This is an extra inch of length, and its purpose is to keep the wood from splitting when you glue and clamp a tight-fitting tenon into the mortise. Leave the horn in place until after glue-up, then saw it off. Some books omit the horn from their mortising recipes, but unless you make joints that are really loose, you need it.
- In some frame-and-panel constructions where the groove that holds the panel runs the full length of the stiles, you will want to add a piece called a haunch. This is a stub of wood on the tenon, and it fills the exposed end of this groove. A haunch is always present on old work because you couldn't make a stopped groove with a hand plough plane. However, if you're able to stop the groove, as when routing or even table-sawing, you don't need to make the haunch.

THE ANATOMY OF A MORTISE-AND-TENON JOINT

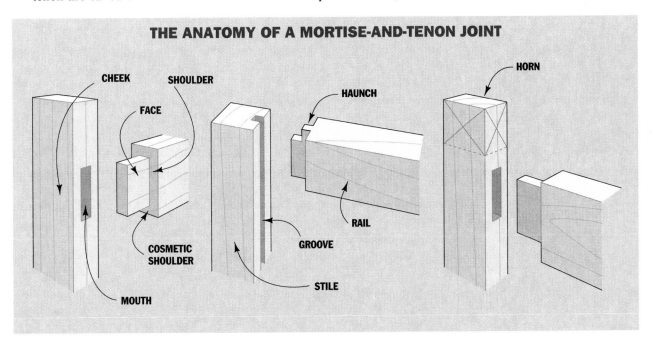

CHEEK · SHOULDER · FACE · HORN · HAUNCH · COSMETIC SHOULDER · RAIL · GROOVE · MOUTH · STILE

Designing a Mortise-and-Tenon Joint

There is no absolute formula for the design of mortise-and-tenon joints. However, there are a number of factors to keep in mind as you're designing a joint for a particular situation. Begin by being clear about the ultimate purpose of the joint—a cabinet door does not bear the stress that a chair must, so its joints don't necessarily have to be as robust.

As a chain can only be as strong as its weakest link, so a mortise-and-tenon joint fails when its weakest part gives up. Therefore, you want to design a balanced joint, where both parts are equally resistant to stress. This means you should attempt to distribute the wood tissue evenly between the two parts of the joint.

TYPICAL MORTISE-AND-TENON DIMENSIONS

ONE-THIRD TO ONE-QUARTER TOTAL WIDTH OF TENON

$1/8$" COSMETIC SHOULDER

$1/16$"–$1/8$" CLEARANCE

ABOUT ONE-HALF OF STILE WIDTH (SOMEWHAT LONGER ON NARROW STILES)

Thickness of Tenon, Width of Mortise

When the two pieces of wood you're joining are the same thickness, divide the thickness roughly in half, as shown in *Tenon Thickness/Mortise Width*. For example, if the wood is an inch thick, make the tenon $1/2$ inch thick and make each tenon cheek $1/4$ inch. That said, you can adjust the dimensions to suit the tools you have. For instance, if your wood is $7/8$ inch thick, the ideal mortise width is $7/16$ inch. But if you don't have that size router bit and have to choose between a $3/8$-inch bit and a $1/2$-inch bit, go with the larger bit.

Length of Tenon, Depth of Mortise

The tenon and the mortise make a cross-grain construction. Normal wood movement acts against the joint, so the deeper the tenon goes into the mortise, the greater the potential for stress. Moisture-induced movement actually may make a joint with a longer tenon weaker than one with a shorter tenon—unless you take the tenon all the way through the stile and wedge it from the other side.

On the other hand, if the tenon isn't long enough, there won't be enough gluing surface. The happy compromise is to mortise about halfway into the stile, as shown in *Typical Mortise-and-Tenon Dimensions*. In narrow stock, go a bit more than halfway. Thus if the stile is 3 inches wide, make the tenon $1\frac{1}{2}$ inches long. But if the stile is only $1\frac{1}{2}$ inches wide, make the tenon about 1 inch long.

How much clearance should you leave at the bottom of the mortise? About $1/16$ inch will accommodate stray chips and excess glue.

How short is too short? Kitchen-cabinet manufacturers get away with a $1/2$-inch stub tenon—one that just fits the panel groove they mill in the edge of rails and stiles. The joint is relatively strong because the manufacturers control the moisture content of the wood very carefully, and they mill the joints to very exacting dimensions—much more precisely than I think can be achieved consistently in a small shop.

Since you probably can't achieve such stunning accuracy without investing a lot of money in industrial equipment, you probably can't get away with a stub tenon as short as theirs. Unless you're working with very small pieces, make your tenons at least $3/4$ inch long.

Width of Tenon, Length of Mortise

When the mortise is not at the end of the stile, make the tenon the full width of the rail, minus $1/8$ inch at each side for a cosmetic shoulder. You must have a shoulder top and

TENON THICKNESS/ MORTISE WIDTH

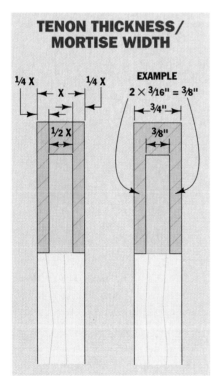

$1/4$ X $1/4$ X   EXAMPLE
$2 \times 3/16$" = $3/8$"
X $3/4$"
$1/2$ X $3/8$"

bottom to conceal any defects in the mortise as well as subsequent shrinkage of the tenon in width, but they don't need to be any larger than ⅛ inch.

When the mortise is at the end of the stile, leave a bit more of an allowance for the cosmetic shoulder nearest the end of the stile— perhaps one-quarter to one-third the total width of the tenon. In general terms, this means the cosmetic shoulder toward the end of the stile will be about ½ inch wide. This will help keep the end of the stile from splitting.

As a rule of thumb, a tenon shouldn't be more than ten times as wide as it is thick. This situation may arise when you are making an entry door or the headboard and posts of a bed. The problem here is wood movement.

Remember, wood moves considerably across the grain and very little along it. The wider a tenon is, the more it will move in relation to the mortised piece, which isn't moving at all. The resulting stress can cause the joint to fail and/or the pieces to crack. If you need a very wide tenon, divide it into two or even more tenons, as shown in *Dividing Wide Tenons*, which helps distribute the cross-grain stress. Space the tenons their own width apart, as shown.

Selecting Wood for Mortise-and-Tenon Joints

For most mortise-and-tenon joints, it doesn't matter how the wood was sawn, as long as the grain is straight. You can choose flat-sawn, rift-sawn, or quarter-sawn material, according to how it

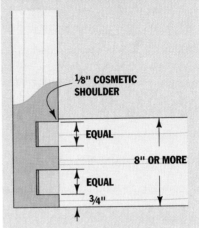

DIVIDING WIDE TENONS

Split one wide tenon into two or more smaller tenons to avoid wood movement troubles.

⅛" COSMETIC SHOULDER

EQUAL

8" OR MORE

EQUAL

¾"

looks and what you have selected for the rest of the project. There is no strength or added stability to be gained in orienting the grain in some particular way.

Milling Stock for Rails and Stiles

When you mill stock for rails and stiles, go for the finished dimension. Don't leave extra to clean up at the end—you won't remove an appreciable amount of wood by smooth planing or sanding.

However, when your design calls for a mortise closer than about an inch from the end of a stile or leg, don't forget to add a horn to the length of the pieces as you're cutting.

Whenever you're making rails and stiles or table legs and aprons, always make one extra of each different piece. This is insurance against error as well as against the possibility that one piece will twist or warp unacceptably. The extra pieces will also help you set up your equipment, make test cuts, and adjust when necessary.

TROUBLESHOOTING

SHORTEN THE TENON

The moisture content of your wood is an important variable when dimensioning the parts of a mortise-and-tenon joint. If the relative humidity in your shop is significantly different than where the furniture is going to live, the joint will be under moisture-induced stress for the rest of its life. You can do two things about it. First, condition your wood yourself, as described in "Storing Your Stock" on page 7. Second, make the tenon somewhat shorter and the mortise somewhat shallower than you otherwise would. This will reduce the amount of wood subject to movement.

THE RIGHT SIZE

A bill of materials may specify the shoulder-to-shoulder length of rails, so make sure you account for the additional length of the tenons.

When working from plans in books, your best insurance is to draw the pieces full sized. Then you can verify dimensions by offering up the pieces directly to the drawing.

Old-timers often lay out dimensions full sized on a stick or on the face of a board. When you want to make a cabinet to fit an exact space, you can avoid error and confusion by making such a stick (sometimes called a story board) from a length of 1 × 2 and marking the actual space on it.

Routing Mortises

In general, you make the mortise first, then you make the tenon to fit, since it is easier to adjust the tenon. You can achieve an excellent result with a variety of different tools, including a router, a hollow chisel on the drill press, a dedicated hollow-chisel mortiser, a slot mortiser, and a mortising chisel.

Routing Mortises

You need a plunge router and a jig to rout mortises. You cannot do it freehand, and even with a jig, it's totally unsafe to try it with a fixed-base, nonplunge router.

For the jig, I recommend the unit shown in "A Simple Mortising Jig." The basic setup is shown in *Routing a Mortise*. Note that a simple system of opposing wedges locks the workpiece against the front of the jig and keeps it butted to the end block.

Use a spiral upcut bit for routing mortises. Its geometry helps to clear the chips, and in many cases, you will be able to go to full depth in one or two passes. A straight-flute cutter requires smaller bites.

When routing, plunge the bit into the workpiece at the right end of the mortise and cut from right to left. This keeps the bit from pushing the edge guide away from the jig.

Routing Mortises Accurately

There's no reason to settle for less than perfect accuracy when making mortises. You want both dimensional accuracy (the right size and location) and geometric accuracy (square and parallel). Here's the process I recommend:

STEP 1 Set up your equipment. Use your extra workpiece for setup and to verify accuracy before you make joints in your good stock.

STEP 2 Rout the mortise in the extra piece to test your setup. Verify the mortise position by measuring the thickness of the cheeks with your dial caliper, as shown in *Verifying*

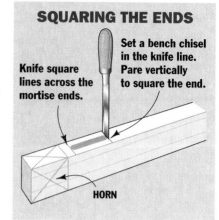

SQUARING THE ENDS

Knife square lines across the mortise ends.

Set a bench chisel in the knife line. Pare vertically to square the end.

HORN

the Setup. If the mortise isn't in the right place, adjust the edge guide.

STEP 3 Verify the length of the mortise. Also, use your combination square to verify that the ends of the mortise are perpendicular to the surface. They probably are, but it is important to habitually check accuracy at every stage. If you don't, you won't know why things go wrong.

STEP 4 Crosscut the test piece, and measure the thickness of the cheeks at the bottom of the mortise. If it's exactly the same as at the

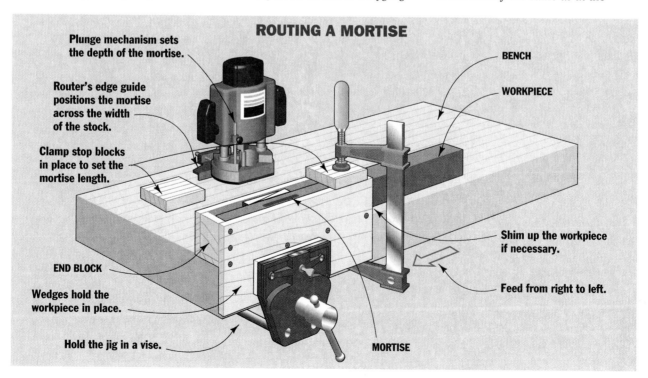

ROUTING A MORTISE

Plunge mechanism sets the depth of the mortise.

Router's edge guide positions the mortise across the width of the stock.

Clamp stop blocks in place to set the mortise length.

END BLOCK

Wedges hold the workpiece in place.

Hold the jig in a vise.

BENCH

WORKPIECE

Shim up the workpiece if necessary.

Feed from right to left.

MORTISE

mouth, the mortise walls will be parallel. If they're not parallel, go over your setup. The problem might simply be a stray chip preventing the workpiece from sitting square.

Squaring the Ends of a Routed Mortise

The router makes a round-end mortise. You could round your tenons to fit, but I think you get a better fit by chiseling the mortise square. To start the cut, push or tap a chisel straight down into the wood. Levering forward breaks the chip and lifts it out.

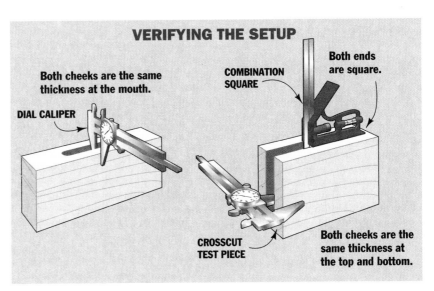

VERIFYING THE SETUP

Both cheeks are the same thickness at the mouth.

DIAL CALIPER

COMBINATION SQUARE

Both ends are square.

CROSSCUT TEST PIECE

Both cheeks are the same thickness at the top and bottom.

SHOP SOLUTIONS: A Simple Mortising Jig

In my mind, jigs should be quick to make and easy to toss when the job is done. That's the thinking behind this jig, which is made from scrap plywood. The exact sizes aren't critical.

Start by making a U-shaped box with a base and two sides into which the workpiece will fit. Add the end block for rigidity and to help locate the workpiece; shims and the folding wedges lock the workpiece in position. The top of the box acts like a guide for the router; blocks clamped to it act like end stops, with the router's own edge guide bearing on the back of the box to steer it in a straight line. The front side of the box extends down so that it can be held in the vise.

Make the box wider and deeper for larger workpieces.

This jig makes use of a handheld plunge router. It provides a means of holding your workpiece in place and a set of guides to restrict the router's travel.

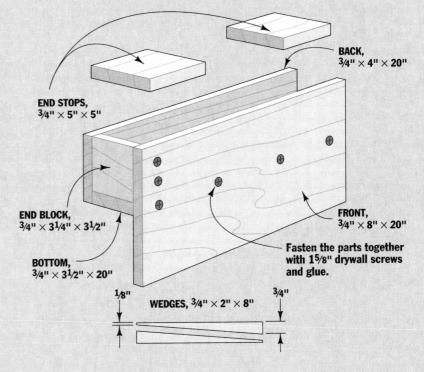

END STOPS, 3/4" × 5" × 5"

BACK, 3/4" × 4" × 20"

END BLOCK, 3/4" × 3 1/4" × 3 1/2"

BOTTOM, 3/4" × 3 1/2" × 20"

FRONT, 3/4" × 8" × 20"

Fasten the parts together with 1 5/8" drywall screws and glue.

1/8"

WEDGES, 3/4" × 2" × 8"

3/4"

Mortising with a Hollow-Chisel Mortiser

A hollow-chisel mortiser, shown in the photos below, is a machine capable of drilling a square hole. The hollow chisel is a square steel tube with a drill bit inside of it. The edges of the tube are sharpened and work in tandem with the bit's cutters.

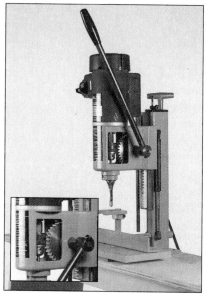

A dedicated hollow-chisel mortiser has a sturdier mechanism than a drill press and can produce more accurate cuts.

A dedicated hollow-chisel mortising machine is much better than the hollow-chisel attachment you can buy for most drill presses. But if the attachment is what you have, you can improve its performance if you take the additional step of drilling out most of the waste with a Forstner bit before you go at it with the hollow chisel.

The reason for this extra step is because driving the square chisel into the work takes great force. The drill press is not designed to withstand this force, and it is liable to flex, resulting in inaccurate mortises. Over time, the stress will add slop to the drill-press mechanism.

Setting Up a Hollow-Chisel Mortiser

It's tricky to set up a hollow-chisel mortiser. To begin with, you must make sure the chisel and the bit are truly sharp.

You can get a sharpening device that's made for honing the inside of a hollow chisel, as shown in the photo below, but you can also hone the inside bevels with a small slip-stone. Remove any burrs, and polish the outside of the chisel by honing it on a flat, fine waterstone. Don't neglect the auger bit. File the cutting lips as you would sharpen a regular bit.

Once the tool is sharp, follow these steps to set up for the cut:

STEP 1 Adjust the hollow chisel so that it's not only perpendicular to the table but also square to the fence. Most drill presses have some rotational play in the quill, which makes squareness difficult to achieve.

STEP 2 Adjust the clearance between the bit and the hollow chisel to about the thickness of a folded business card. It may seem easier to mortise if the clearance is larger, but the bit is liable to wobble inaccurately.

STEP 3 Set the speed of the drill press according to the density of the wood and the width of the chisel. Start in the middle of the low speed range. If the chisel packs up with chips, try a different speed, either faster or slower. You'll know everything is set correctly when you can go to the full depth of the mortise in one punch.

STEP 4 Install hold-downs, as shown in *Hollow-Chisel Mortising*, or you won't be able to withdraw the chisel from the wood. Use a stop block so that at least one end of the mortise will be consistently located.

STEP 5 Cut the mortise. The chisel cuts most accurately when balanced by wood on all four sides of it

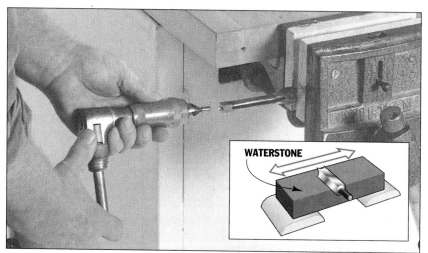

WATERSTONE

Hone the inside of the hollow chisel with a plug-style sharpener, driven by a bit brace. The sharpener comes with several pilot plugs to fit different-sized chisels. Hone the sides of the hollow chisel on a fine, flat stone.

or on two opposing sides. It drifts when there is wood on only three sides because the forces involved aren't balanced.

Therefore, cut the ends of the mortise first, as shown in *Sequence of Cuts*. Then stab in between, leaving webs of wood that are narrower than the chisel. Finally, cut away the webs.

FACT OR FICTION

DRILLING MORTISES?

While it's possible to drill a mortise with the drill press and then pare the cheeks flat with a bench chisel, the cheeks are almost certain to be unparallel. Inaccuracy here means your framed panel or door won't be flat or square, and the glue will have lousy surfaces to bond with.

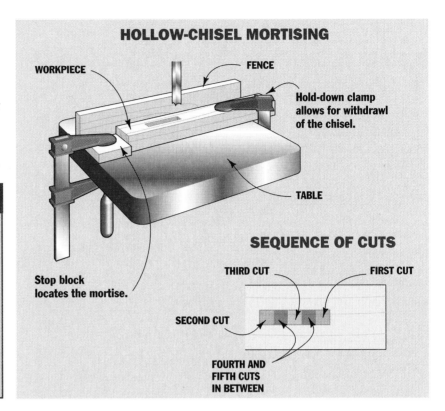

HOLLOW-CHISEL MORTISING

WORKPIECE
FENCE
Hold-down clamp allows for withdrawl of the chisel.
TABLE
Stop block locates the mortise.

SEQUENCE OF CUTS

THIRD CUT
FIRST CUT
SECOND CUT
FOURTH AND FIFTH CUTS IN BETWEEN

Problem Solving
Hollow-Chisel Woes

Hollow-chisel mortisers work well, provided they are set up correctly. It will probably take some fine-tuning and experimentation to get yours up to speed.

PROBLEM	SOLUTION
The hollow chisel sticks in the wood, and I have to fight to withdraw it.	Work the outside of the hollow chisel on your fine sharpening stone to remove any burrs and to polish it smooth. Ideally, the chisel should be minutely larger at the cutting end and taper back slightly toward the shank, so bear down on the shank end as you're honing.
Help! My chisel makes an earsplitting shrill noise, and there's a wisp of smoke.	The auger is rubbing against the hollow chisel. Make sure it's properly seated in the drill chuck, reset the gap, and tighten down the chuck hard. If this doesn't solve the problem, you may have bent the auger, which you can't fix. Replace it.
The bottom of the mortise is such a ragged mess that the tenon doesn't go home.	The auger probably protrudes too far beyond the end of the hollow chisel. Make the gap smaller. You can clean up a rough mortise with a hand chisel, but if you set the hollow chisel right, you won't have to.

Making Tenons

You have a number of choices for how you make tenons: on a table saw, on a band saw, with a router, or with hand tools. With all of these except the router, making a tenon is a two-step operation. You cut the shoulders, then the faces (or vice versa).

Given a choice, I prefer to cut both the tenon shoulders and the faces on the table saw. But I know other craftsmen who make the shoulder cuts on the table saw, then move to the band saw to cut the faces. Whatever technique you choose, your objective doesn't change. You're trying to make a tenon with the characteristics shown in *Tenon Considerations*.

You can't achieve these objectives if you are casual about milling the wood in the first place. As pieces of a project must all be the same size, ends and edges must be square to one another, and parallel edges must be parallel. This is because in order to make the tenon, you must set stops and gauges in contact with the original square faces of the workpiece. If the stops and gauges aren't right, the tenon won't be right either.

Checking a Tenon for Accuracy

Just as you used a dial caliper to check the mortise for accuracy, you can measure the tenon. To verify that it's parallel, lay a straightedge on the face of the workpiece and gauge the distance to the tenon at its root and at its end. You can even check it for twist—make yourself a pair of 6-inch-long winding sticks. Set one stick on the face of the workpiece

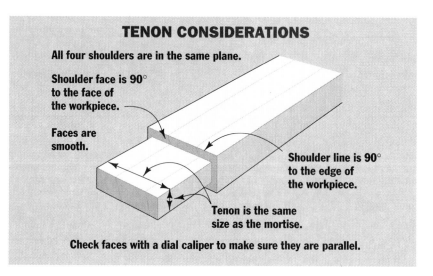

TENON CONSIDERATIONS

All four shoulders are in the same plane.

Shoulder face is 90° to the face of the workpiece.

Faces are smooth.

Shoulder line is 90° to the edge of the workpiece.

Tenon is the same size as the mortise.

Check faces with a dial caliper to make sure they are parallel.

and the other on the face of the tenon, and sight the two sticks.

How Tight to Tenon?

You should be able to push most of the tenon home by leaning down on it or by lightly tapping it with a mallet. The final closing may need moderate pressure with a clamp, but if you have to use extreme force, it's too tight. With a too-tight joint, you may hear the wood tick as it tries to comply, but the next sound you hear will be the crack of splitting wood.

Don't forget that glue has its own thickness, which the joint has to accommodate. Plus glue also introduces moisture. It only takes seconds for the moisture in the glue to penetrate the surface of the tenon and make it $1/1000$ inch bigger. The drier the wood, the faster it swells.

Table-Sawing Tenons

When table-sawing tenons, the process starts with the shoulders. Use a miter gauge to guide the work, and gauge the tenon length against a block of

wood clamped to the rip fence, as shown in *Cutting Tenon Shoulders*.

Screw a wooden auxiliary fence onto the face of the miter gauge. The fence supports the workpiece right up to the blade and increases the heft of the gauge, helping it slide. A little oil wiped into the miter gauge slot will help, too. Then saw the shoulders as follows:

STEP 1 Set the blade to the exact depth of the shoulder—there's no point in trying to sneak up on it.

FACT OR FICTION

TENONING WITH A DADO HEAD?

A common method of removing the waste from tenon cheeks is to make repeated crosscut passes with a dado head in the table saw. You will get a shape that looks like a tenon, but the surface left by a dado head is neither flat nor smooth. It's not accurate, and it won't glue well. Tenons made by repeatedly crosscutting dadoes on the radial-arm saw are also liable to be inaccurate because of flexing between the arm, carriage, and table.

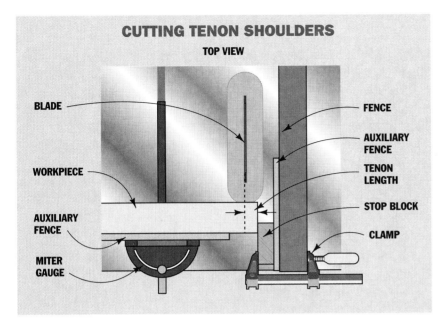

CUTTING TENON SHOULDERS

TOP VIEW

BLADE

WORKPIECE

AUXILIARY FENCE

MITER GAUGE

FENCE

AUXILIARY FENCE

TENON LENGTH

STOP BLOCK

CLAMP

STEP 2 Set the miter gauge absolutely square. If you have any doubt about the ability of the gauge to hold the setting, make yourself a sliding crosscut box, as shown in "Crosscutting on the Table Saw" on page 18.

STEP 3 Set the stop block on the rip fence to the precise length of the tenon as measured from the outside edge of the blade. If you're using a crosscut box, clamp a stop block to its fence.

STEP 4 Cut a test piece to verify dimensions, then cut all of the tenon shoulders with everything at the same setting.

STEP 5 Change the depth setting, if necessary, to cut the cosmetic shoulders. Keep everything else the same.

I find that a good-quality alternate-top-bevel (ATB), carbide-tipped blade makes a sharp, clean shoulder. The number of teeth doesn't matter.

Cutting the Faces

To cut tenon faces on the table saw, stand up the workpiece vertically and use a fixture to carry it past the blade. It is totally unsafe (as well as inaccurate) to do this operation freehand. You can easily make your own fixture, as shown in *A Simple Tenoning Fixture*.

Clamp the workpiece to the fixture with two clamps, as shown in the photo. Place the fixture next to the blade, and set the blade height so the teeth just reach the shoulder cut. Hold the fixture against the fence, and position the fence for the first cut. Keep pressing the fixture tight to the fence as you make the cut. Verify the setup, then make the first cut on all of the pieces. Move the fence over and repeat for the second cut.

Contractor-style table saws may not have enough power to cut the full length of the tenon into end grain in a single pass. Rather than bogging the saw, which makes the blade flutter inaccurately and also overheats the motor, simply make two or more passes. A good 24-tooth, ATB, carbide-tipped rip blade will minimize the problem.

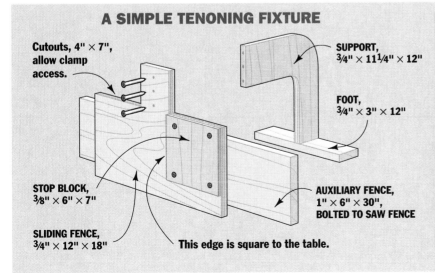

A SIMPLE TENONING FIXTURE

Cutouts, 4" × 7", allow clamp access.

SUPPORT, ¾" × 11¼" × 12"

FOOT, ¾" × 3" × 12"

STOP BLOCK, ⅜" × 6" × 7"

SLIDING FENCE, ¾" × 12" × 18"

This edge is square to the table.

AUXILIARY FENCE, 1" × 6" × 30", BOLTED TO SAW FENCE

Press the fixture firmly against the rip fence, and always hold the workpiece with two clamps.

Band-Sawing Tenon Faces

The band saw is a good alternative to the table saw for cutting tenon faces. In fact, it is my tool of choice when tenoning large pieces that would be awkward to hold on end on the table saw.

For these cuts, equip your band saw with a ½- or ¼-inch sharp, skip-tooth blade, with three or four teeth per inch. Note that the machine must be well tuned to cut smooth faces you can glue straight from the saw. Now you have two choices.

If you're only cutting a few tenons, lay them out individually, as described in "Laying Out a Mortise-and-Tenon Joint" on page 56. Then band-saw the tenons freehand, as shown in the photo.

If you have multiple tenons to cut, it will pay to set up a fence and a stop block. Table-saw the shoulders first, then make the face cuts, as

When band-sawing tenons freehand, lay out the tenons on the stock, then band-saw the faces before table-sawing the shoulders. This way, the waste will remain attached, preserving your layout lines.

shown in *Band-Sawing Tenon Faces.*

Though it is tempting to band-saw the tenon shoulders as well as the faces, don't. The table saw makes a much crisper cut.

Routing Tenons

Unlike other methods, the router allows you to make the tenon shoulder and face in one operation. On the other hand, you'll need four setups to rout all the way around.

You can rout tenons with a fixed-base or a plunge router. Use a pattern-cutting bit, preferably one with at least a ¾-inch diameter so you can go to full depth in one pass.

Clamp your pieces together side by side, and knife shoulder lines across their faces. Clamp the pieces to your bench with a straightedge, as shown in *Routing Tenons.* The side of the straightedge should align perfectly with the shoulder line. Set the depth of cut to control the tenon's thickness. Rout the tenons by guiding the bit along the straightedge. Turn the pieces over and clamp them together again to rout the

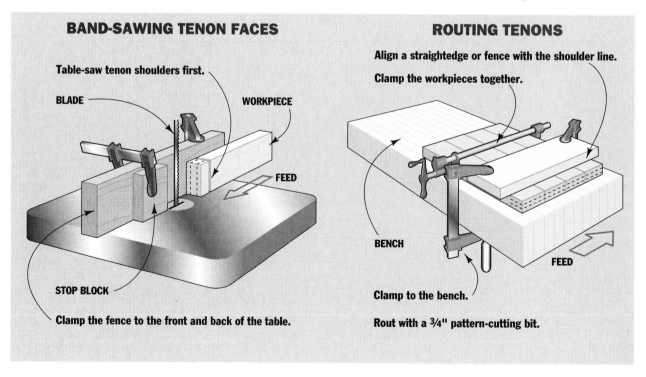

BAND-SAWING TENON FACES

Table-saw tenon shoulders first.

BLADE

WORKPIECE

FEED

STOP BLOCK

Clamp the fence to the front and back of the table.

ROUTING TENONS

Align a straightedge or fence with the shoulder line.

Clamp the workpieces together.

BENCH

FEED

Clamp to the bench.

Rout with a ¾" pattern-cutting bit.

second face. Then clamp them face to face to cut the tenons to width and to make the cosmetic shoulders.

Assembling the Joint

There's very little you can do to adjust a structure once it's glued and clamped. Always test fit the entire construction, then check it as follows:

- Lay a straightedge across the joints to check the alignment of the mating surfaces. It's possible to skew the alignment by sloppy clamping, so move the clamps, and see if the problem persists.

- Check the corners for square-ness. If the frame is not square, a poorly dimensioned piece or a skewed clamp may be the cause.
- Measure between the rails at each end of the frame. Tenons often aren't quite tight in width, so the tenoned piece has a little room to float. Add clamps to pull the pieces into line.
- Measure the diagonals to make sure they are equal.

Gluing a Mortise and Tenon

Always brush glue on all four faces of the tenon and on all four walls of the mortise. But don't put glue on the shoulders of the tenon or outside the mouth of the mortise.

Fit the parts together and clamp the construction. Repeat the checks you made during the test assembly. You can make minor adjustments in alignment and squareness by fiddling with the placement and tightness of the clamps.

Allow the assembly to sit for about 30 minutes. If the joints are tight, the hydraulic pressure inside the joints will make the mortise cheeks belly outward.

Remove the clamps and eliminate any belly by setting a C-clamp with protective blocks across the face of each joint.

Problem Solving
Mortise-and-Tenon Troubles

Since everything happens inside a mortise-and-tenon joint, you may have trouble seeing why the joint doesn't fit exactly right. Here is some advice on fixing some of the more common problems.

PROBLEM	SOLUTION
The joint is too loose.	You can make a tenon bigger by gluing on pieces of wood. Don't try to add a thin shim because you won't be able to get it right. Instead, glue a piece that's big enough to saw into, then re-mark and recut the tenon.
The joint is too tight.	Even if the mortise is the culprit, it's easier and more accurate to pare the tenon to fit. Mark how much wood you are trying to remove. Set the piece in the vise, and use a wide bench chisel to pare horizontally, across the grain.
Everything is the right size, but the tenon won't go all the way home.	First, see whether there are any stray chips in the bottom of the mortise. Next, check the tenon shoulders. If one of the shoulders isn't clean, pare it with a bench chisel. Finally, check the depth of the mortise. If you can't rout or chop it any deeper, you can always saw the tenon a little bit short.
The joint fits together, but the faces of the pieces don't line up.	If the error is less than about $1/32$ inch, glue up, then plane the step away with a smooth plane. If the misalignment is more than about $1/32$ inch, remove material from either the mortise or the tenon to make the necessary shift. Keep in mind that you'll probably have to add the same amount of material to the opposite side of the joint to compensate. It may be easier to make a new part.

Hand Cutting a Mortise-and-Tenon Joint

Teaching yourself how to make a mortise-and-tenon joint by hand will start you on the road to general proficiency with marking tools, a handsaw, and a chisel. As a bonus, you're in for a real thrill the first time you fit a handmade joint.

When you work by machine, once you're set up, you don't lay out every cut. When you work by hand, however, the process begins with accurate layout of every cut on both parts of each joint. Then you chop the mortise to the size of the chisel you have, saw the tenon to match, and fit the joint together.

The conventional tenon saw (top) cuts on the push stroke, while the Japanese ryoba saw (bottom) cuts on the pull stroke. The ryoba saw has two sets of teeth—coarse for ripping and fine for crosscutting.

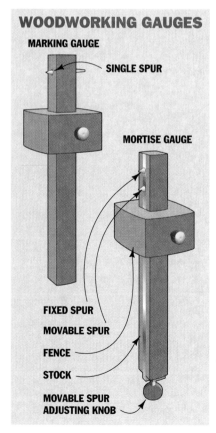

WOODWORKING GAUGES

MARKING GAUGE

SINGLE SPUR

MORTISE GAUGE

FIXED SPUR

MOVABLE SPUR

FENCE

STOCK

MOVABLE SPUR ADJUSTING KNOB

The Necessary Tools

You'll need some basic hand tools to cut this joint, and you'll find other uses in your shop for many of them. The nice thing about hand tools is that even the very best ones aren't terribly expensive, especially when compared to the price of machinery. About $400 will buy you a set, with which you can make almost any kind of furniture. Specifically for a mortise-and-tenon joint you'll need the following:

- **Mortise gauge.** As shown in *Woodworking Gauges,* a mortise gauge has two spurs, one fixed and one movable. The fence slides along the stock for adjustment. You set the spurs to the width of the mortise chisel, then set the fence to the thickness of the mortise cheek. The spurs come sharp like a pencil. Leave them that way.
- **Marking gauge.** A marking gauge has a single spur, also sharpened like a pencil. A third gauge, not shown, is a cutting gauge, which has a knife in

place of the spur. It's used in dovetailing.
- **Marking knife.** A marking knife is used with a try square to cut a line across the grain. The knife should be sharpened as a vee, without a secondary bevel. I use a Swiss army knife because it has a thin blade of good steel and feels right in my hand. The knives usually sold for marking out have a thick blade and are difficult to sharpen. An X-Acto knife is too thin and too flexible.
- **Try square.** A try square, with fixed blade and stock, is the woodworker's traditional tool for laying out lines across the grain. This tool is perfectly adequate for laying out most joints; however, many people have replaced it with a combination square, which is more versatile. You need a 12-inch combination square, and it's good to have one with a 4-inch blade as well.
- **Tenon saw.** The traditional tenon saw is a backsaw between 10 and 14 inches long, with 12

or 14 teeth per inch. One around 10 inches long will be easiest to control. The Japanese *ryoba* saw is also an excellent tenon saw. Get a 12-inch saw with 14 teeth per inch on the crosscut side. (The other side has coarser teeth for ripping.) Japanese saws cut on the pull stroke, which takes a little getting used to. The two styles are shown in the photo.

- **Mortise chisel.** A mortise chisel is designed to be pounded into the wood, then levered out, so it has to be thick and sturdy, as shown in *Woodworking Chisels.* The blade should be rectangular in section and as deep or deeper than it is wide. There should be no narrow neck where the blade enters the handle. Usually there's a ferrule atop the handle to keep it from splitting under impact.

You'll need a specific size chisel for each width of mortise you intend to cut. If you are going to buy just one mortise chisel and furniture is what you are making, get the ³⁄₈-inch size. Build your collection of chisels in increments of ¹⁄₁₆ inch on either side of ³⁄₈ inch. Make sure the cross-section of the chisel is square. If it is not, reject it.

Mortising is easy with a good chisel and virtually impossible with a bad one. It is one of the few operations where lousy tools could well be the reason you can't do it well.

- **Joiner's mallet.** A true joiner's mallet has a flat head with angled faces, so it follows your arm and strikes true and square. If you can't find one, it's worth making one like that shown in *A Joiner's Mallet.* Use a hard, dense wood such as maple or beech. If necessary, you can laminate the head from thinner pieces of wood.

- **Sawing board.** A sawing board, sometimes called a bench hook, provides a stop to hold the workpiece against as you cut it. It's an essential accessory for working wood by hand that is

easily made from some scraps, as shown in *A Sawing Board;* the one on the left will work with both English and Japanese saws.

- **Cutting board.** A cutting board protects the bench top when you chop downward with a chisel. If you make it the same thickness and general dimensions as the sawing board, you can also use it to support long stock for sawing.

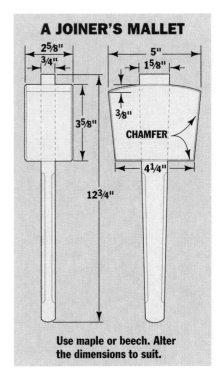

A JOINER'S MALLET

2⅝"
¾"
5"
1⅝"
3⅝"
⅜"
CHAMFER
4¼"
12¾"

Use maple or beech. Alter the dimensions to suit.

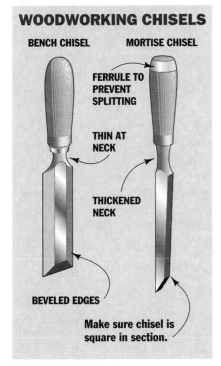

WOODWORKING CHISELS

BENCH CHISEL   MORTISE CHISEL

FERRULE TO PREVENT SPLITTING

THIN AT NECK

THICKENED NECK

BEVELED EDGES

Make sure chisel is square in section.

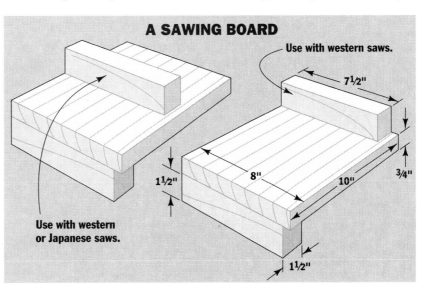

A SAWING BOARD

Use with western saws.

7½"

Use with western or Japanese saws.

1½"

8"

10"

¾"

1½"

Laying Out the Joint

On the tenon piece, usually the horizontal rail, the key dimension is the between-shoulders distance. On the mortise piece, usually the vertical stile, the key dimension is the distance between the mortises.

"Laying out a Mortise-and-Tenon Joint" shows you the process, step-by-step. But here are a few other points to consider as you work:

● Always verify the shoulder-to-shoulder distance on the first tenon piece by measuring or by

STEP-BY-STEP: LAYING OUT A MORTISE-AND-TENON JOINT

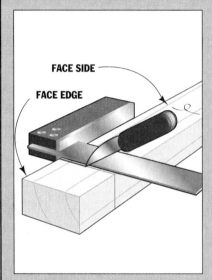

STEP 1 Knife the shoulder line for the tenon on all four surfaces, working from the face side and edge.

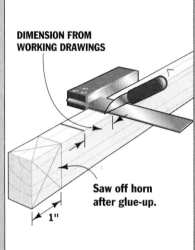

STEP 2 Knife the length of the mortise.

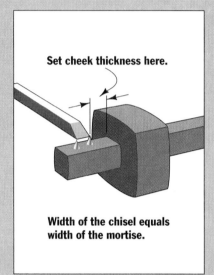

STEP 3 Set the mortise gauge for both the width of the mortise and the thickness of the cheek.

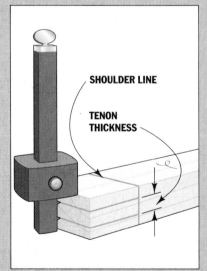

STEP 4 Mark the tenon thickness with the mortise gauge.

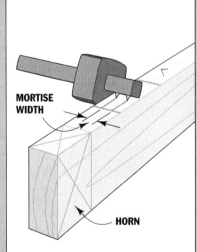

STEP 5 Mark the mortise width with the same setting.

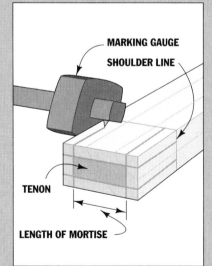

STEP 6 Mark the cosmetic shoulders with the marking gauge.

offering the piece to your full-sized drawing. Then use this first piece as a template, and knife the shoulder lines on all of the other tenon pieces.

- If you are making stiles, locate and knife both ends of all of the mortises, verifying the measurement from the full-sized drawing as with the tenon pieces.
- If you are making legs for a table, cut the bottom end of each leg square, and measure up to locate the mortises. Cut away the horn above the mortise

after you fit and glue the joint.

- If the mortises will go all the way through the workpiece, mark the show side of the wood with light lines and cuts. If you set these lines in deeply, you'll never be able to plane them out.
- Select your wood with care. While a router can make a clean cut through gnarly grain without hesitating, trying to make the same cut with a chisel is no fun at all. You'll get the best results in very plain, straight-grained wood.

USING A MORTISE GAUGE

Making a clean, straight pair of lines with a mortise gauge depends not on strength but on how you grip the tool. The basic action is a push away from you, which you repeat several times while rolling the spurs into the wood.

STEP 1 Place three fingers around the stock, your index finger over the fence, and your thumb directly behind the marking spurs, so it can push.

STEP 2 Trap the work between your body and a bench stop, or lay it on the bench, so you can hold the work steady.

STEP 3 Bring the gauge into position, but turn it so the spurs don't contact the wood. Use the inside edge of your middle finger to press the fence into contact with the workpiece.

STEP 4 Push the gauge forward with a flowing motion, still without making a mark. Repeat without marking until you have the feel of the motion.

STEP 5 Roll your wrist so that the spurs just touch the work at a low angle, then repeat the motion.

STEP 6 Make two or three light passes, one right on top of the other.

Both mortise gauges and marking gauges are held in the same manner, with all of your fingers involved. Use your middle finger to maintain contact between the gauge and workpiece, and use your thumb and index finger to roll the spurs into the work.

Chopping Mortises

Chopping a mortise with a mallet and chisel is a motion as old as history—ancient Japanese scrolls and Egyptian temple frescoes show it being done in exactly the same way. Basically, you drive the chisel into the wood vertically, then lever the chips out. You make the mortise straight from the chisel; there's no way to improve it by shaving or paring. The exact process is described here; if you do it this way, you will succeed.

STEP 1 Clear the workbench of everything but the workpiece, mallet and chisel, and try square or small combination square.

STEP 2 Place the workpiece on a solid part of the bench, preferably over a leg and absolutely not in the vise. (The shock of mortising would not only overpower the grip of the vise but it would also destroy the vise's accuracy.)

STEP 3 Use two hands to position the chisel between the gauge lines about ¼ inch from the far end of the mortise, as shown in *Chopping a Mortise.* (Don't start at the end of the mortise, or you'll damage it as you lever out the waste.)

STEP 4 Grip the chisel in your left hand (if you are right-handed) and stand back at arm's length. Square up your body, with feet comfortably apart, and sight the chisel vertical.

If you aren't confident in your sense of vertical, put a mirror in front of the setup. This reference will make all the difference.

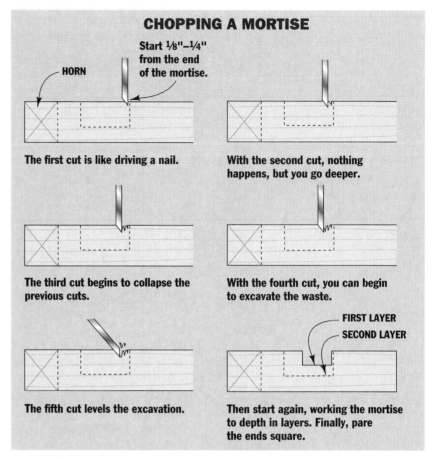

CHOPPING A MORTISE

Start ⅛"–¼" from the end of the mortise.

HORN

The first cut is like driving a nail.

With the second cut, nothing happens, but you go deeper.

The third cut begins to collapse the previous cuts.

With the fourth cut, you can begin to excavate the waste.

FIRST LAYER
SECOND LAYER

The fifth cut levels the excavation.

Then start again, working the mortise to depth in layers. Finally, pare the ends square.

STEP 5 Give the chisel a little whack with the mallet to set it in place, then deliver two solid blows. This first cut will be an incision that crushes the wood fibers without much penetration.

STEP 6 Lift the chisel out of the wood by levering it away from you. Put the mallet down and hold the workpiece down as you lift.

STEP 7 Position the chisel as before, but ⅛ inch closer to you. Set it and whack it again with two solid blows. The second cut will go deeper but still won't raise a chip. Repeat. By the fourth cut or so, you will be deep into the wood, and you will be removing waste when you lever out the chisel.

STEP 8 Chop a full-length trench to shallow but uniform depth, then repeat the trenching operation until you reach full depth. You may ream some extra width into the mortise as you go, but you can compensate by making the tenon a little thicker.

STEP 9 Work to within about ⅛ inch of the ends of the mortise. Clean up the bottom of the mortise before you pare the ends; otherwise, you'll crush the tissue at the mouth of the mortise as you lever the chisel out of the cut.

STEP 10 To pare the ends of the mortise, set the chisel right in the knife marks and drive it straight down. Don't undercut—make the ends truly square to provide the joint with as much strength as possible. Check with your small combination square or a small rule, and make sure you've excavated to full depth right at the ends.

Hand Sawing Tenons

Hand sawing accurate tenons is a function of how you scribe the layout lines and whether your mortise grows as you cut it. Check the tenon piece against the completed mortise to verify the layout. Making the tenon fit perfectly may mean leaving the line, splitting it, or removing it.

In your basic sawing stance, one foot should be in front of the other. Stand where you can sight down your arm to the gauge line on the work. You should be able to see the line and pump your arm without banging your elbow into your body. Saw the tenon as explained in "Sawing a Tenon."

STEP-BY-STEP: SAWING A TENON

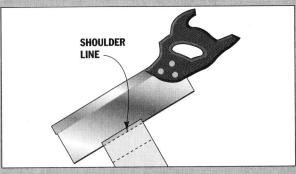

SHOULDER LINE

STEP 1 Hold the wood at an angle in the vise, and start the saw across the end of the wood to establish a kerf.

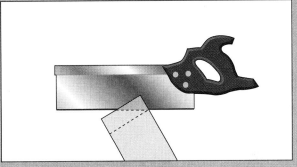

STEP 2 Lower your angle of attack so the saw moves down the near line toward the shoulder line.

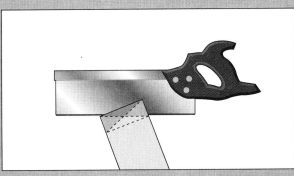

STEP 3 Turn the wood over in the vise. Set the saw in the established kerf, and saw down to the shoulder line.

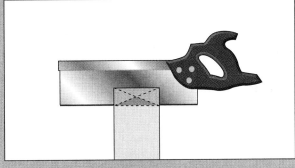

STEP 4 Stand the wood upright in the vise. Saw straight down to the shoulder line. Check that you've sawn to the full depth on both sides.

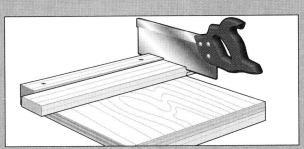

STEP 5 Cut the shoulders on the sawing board, sawing as level and as close to the knife line as you can.

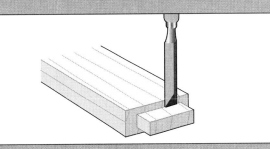

STEP 6 Pare the shoulders to the line with a sharp, wide chisel.

5
MORTISE-AND-TENON
VARIATIONS

Key Ingredients

The mortise-and-tenon joint is such a workhorse that it exists in innumerable variations such as the knock-down tusk tenon joint shown in the photo. In this chapter, I'll detail some of the more common and more useful variations, two of which have come about due to advances in technology.

Thanks to the advent of the high-speed plunge router, you can mortise into the end grain of wood. This permits mortising both parts of the joint and connecting them with a third piece, the loose tenon. Joining wood this way is fast because it relies on just a single router setup to cut both pieces. It is particularly advantageous when joining parts that require angled shoulders since the shoulder cut can be made in one pass of the saw.

Biscuit, or plate, joinery takes the idea a step further. Rather than mortising both pieces, a biscuit joiner cuts matching slots in the mating surfaces. Then a compressed wood "biscuit" is inserted to bridge the joint, much like the tenon in a conventional joint. Originally developed for furniture repair, this system was then extended to join plywood and other man-made boards. Finally

The mortise and tenon offers many decorative and structural possibilities, such as this tusk tenon, a knock-down joint.

it made the jump into solid-wood constructions.

Mortise-and-tenon joints are also modified to accommodate profiles on the edges of rails and stiles when the edges of the pieces aren't cut square. This might happen when a groove or rabbet is cut in the inside edges of the rails and stiles to hold a panel. The groove or rabbet must stop short of the joint, or else the joint must be modified to fit the shape, as shown in *The Long-and-*

Short-Shouldered Mortise and Tenon on page 74.

The same thing happens when you profile the edge of a frame with a decorative molding. There are several ways to accommodate the shape of the molding and to keep it from interfering with the basic geometry of the mortise-and-tenon joint.

Finally, this versatile joint gives rise to a number of three-way variations, where several parts come together at one place.

Making a Through-Wedged Joint

Taking the tenon through the mortise piece and wedging it on the show side adds strength to the joint and visual interest. To achieve maximum strength and appearance, it's important to cut the wedges accurately to a specific size and to make an accurate space for them. Begin by making the through mortise and tenon. Then modify the pieces to accept wedges as follows:

STEP 1 Make a saw cut to accommodate the wedge down each edge of the tenon. The cut should be located as shown in *The Wedged Mortise and Tenon.* If you make the cut too close to the tenon edge, the wood is liable to crack at the root instead of bending.

STEP 2 Make wedges about one and a half times the length of the tenon with a slope of about 1:8. The extra length allows for mushrooming when you drive the wedge home.

STEP 3 Pare both ends of the mortise with a mortise or bench chisel to accommodate the wedges.

STEP 4 Glue and clamp the construction, as shown in *Clamping a Wedged Joint.* Brush glue onto the wedges and tap them home with a steel hammer, taking care not to crush them. Remove the bar clamps—the joint will stay put— and tighten a C-clamp with clamping blocks across the cheeks of the mortise to keep them from bulging out from the hydraulic pressure of the glue.

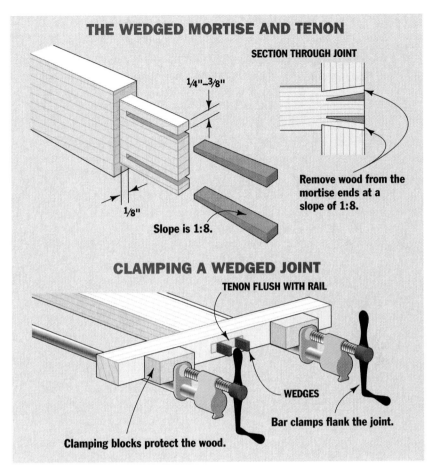

THE WEDGED MORTISE AND TENON

SECTION THROUGH JOINT

1/4"–3/8"

1/8"

Slope is 1:8.

Remove wood from the mortise ends at a slope of 1:8.

CLAMPING A WEDGED JOINT

TENON FLUSH WITH RAIL

WEDGES

Bar clamps flank the joint.

Clamping blocks protect the wood.

STEP 5 When the glue has set, cut the wedges flush with the end of the tenon and clean up. If you've done it right, both wedges should be the same size, there should be no gaps, and there should be no

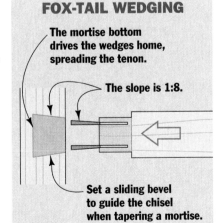

FOX-TAIL WEDGING

The mortise bottom drives the wedges home, spreading the tenon.

The slope is 1:8.

Set a sliding bevel to guide the chisel when tapering a mortise.

evidence of crushed wood on the end grain of the tenon.

Fox-Tail Wedging

The fox-wedged joint is the stopped version of the through-wedged mortise and tenon, as shown in *Fox-Tail Wedging.* You make it in exactly the same way you make the through joint, except the mortises don't go all the way through, and you start the wedges into their kerfs as you insert the tenons into the mortises. As you clamp the joint home, the bottom of the mortise drives the wedges into the kerfs, spreading the tenon.

Making a Loose-Tenon Joint

In this joint, both pieces receive identical mortises, which are filled by a third, tenon-shaped piece of wood, as shown in *The Loose-Tenon Joint*. When the tenon has been glued into the end of the rail, it behaves exactly as if it grew there. The joint is the same size as a regular mortise and tenon, and it is just as strong.

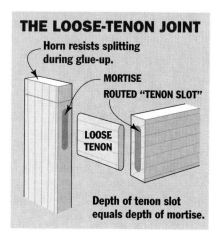

THE LOOSE-TENON JOINT

Horn resists splitting during glue-up.

MORTISE

ROUTED "TENON SLOT"

LOOSE TENON

Depth of tenon slot equals depth of mortise.

The loose-tenon joint has the tremendous advantage of requiring only one basic setup for both parts. You just mortise everything with the same size and depth mortise. Make these mortises with the fixture shown in *A Fixture for Loose Tenoning*. Clamp the pieces in the fixture and rout the mortises, as shown in the photo.

Mortising into End Grain

Spiral-fluted router bits are best for mortising into end grain. Be sure to specify spiral upcut bits, which lift the chips out of the mortise. If you have a choice, get a two-flute cutter.

A hand-held plunge router doesn't have sufficient power to mortise end grain in one pass, but it is capable of plunging a round hole to full depth. You'll get the best results if you plunge one end of the mortise and then the other end to full depth, then make a series of light passes to remove the waste between these two holes.

Making Loose Tenons

Routed mortises have round ends. While it's possible to square the ends of the mortises, it's a lot easier to round the edges of a loose tenon. Saw and plane a board to the appropriate tenon width and thickness. Then round the edges with a roundover bit in a table-mounted router and saw to length. Most people who use loose-tenon joinery establish a few standard widths and thicknesses, so they can machine a lot of tenon stock at one time.

It's best to make your tenons from the same species as the rails and stiles, but if you make up tenon stock ahead of time, that's not always possible. In that case, I'd use a mild hardwood like soft maple, which machines smoothly and glues

Mortising into end grain is no different than mortising edge grain—provided you can hold the stock securely while you rout.

well. But for a large job, in red oak for example, I'd make up a batch of red oak tenons.

Gluing Loose-Tenon Joints

Don't glue the loose tenon into the end grain of the rails before assembly. If you do, you'll have glue squeeze-out to remove, which

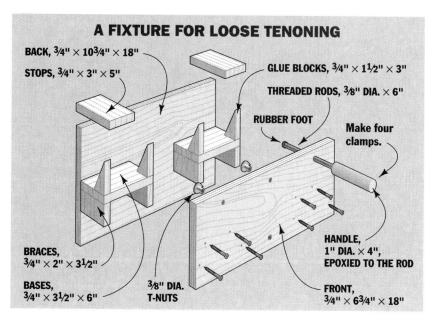

A FIXTURE FOR LOOSE TENONING

BACK, 3/4" × 10 3/4" × 18"

STOPS, 3/4" × 3" × 5"

GLUE BLOCKS, 3/4" × 1 1/2" × 3"

THREADED RODS, 3/8" DIA. × 6"

RUBBER FOOT

Make four clamps.

BRACES, 3/4" × 2" × 3 1/2"

BASES, 3/4" × 3 1/2" × 6"

3/8" DIA. T-NUTS

HANDLE, 1" DIA. × 4", EPOXIED TO THE ROD

FRONT, 3/4" × 6 3/4" × 18"

is extra work at best and which could prevent the tenon shoulders from seating correctly. You'll get a better result if you glue everything at once. Be sure to wet every part of the joint by brushing glue into the mortises as well as onto the tenons. Once everything is square and tight, add C-clamps across the thickness of the joints to make sure there's no glue-induced bellying, as shown in *Squeezing the Joints*.

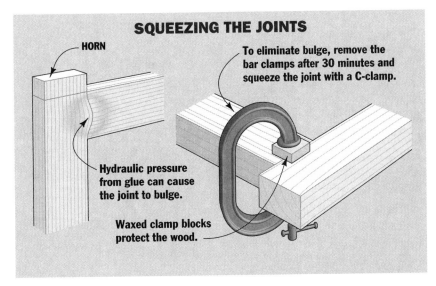

SQUEEZING THE JOINTS

HORN

To eliminate bulge, remove the bar clamps after 30 minutes and squeeze the joint with a C-clamp.

Hydraulic pressure from glue can cause the joint to bulge.

Waxed clamp blocks protect the wood.

Making a Dowel Joint

A dowel joint is a loose tenon with a narrow face—so narrow that you don't get any long-grain gluing surface. Furniture manufacturers rely on dowels to make rail joints, but they have very accurate equipment and can control the precise size and orientation of the holes, as well as the moisture content of the wood and dowels. You probably won't have as much success.

Nevertheless, many commercial doweling jigs exist, and with care, you can make workable dowel joints. You must use a jig, and you must follow the jig's setup and alignment instructions to locate the holes.

Alternatively, you can make accurate dowel holes with the same plunge-router setup you would use to make loose-tenon joints. Simply plunge the extremities of the mortises, but don't waste the web of wood in between. If your setup is accurate, you'll be able to make a satisfactory joint. Here are some other pointers:

● Always use a minimum of two dowels for each joint, spaced about an inch apart, as shown in *Dowel Joinery*.
● Use dowels manufactured for joinery. Don't cut short bits off smooth dowel rods sold at the lumberyard—they're not true in diameter. You can buy spiral-

TROUBLESHOOTING

MORTISES IN END GRAIN
If your plunge-routed mortises have scalloped sides, or chatter marks, you're probably trying to eat too much wood at a single time. Plunge the ends of the mortise to full depth, but try lighter passes (about ¼ inch or so) to remove the web of wood in between.

fluted or splined dowels. The splined ones are slightly oversized, and the spline tips are sharp, so they dig into the sides of the hole and hold tenaciously. The splines, or flutes, also permit excess glue to escape from the joint.
● Choose dowels that fit so tightly that you have to tap them in.
● Brush glue onto the dowel as well as into the hole. Both pieces have to be wet with glue.
● Ensure the joint by tapping a pair of brads through the face of the wood and into the dowel. When the glue lets go, as it eventually will, the brads will hold the construction together.

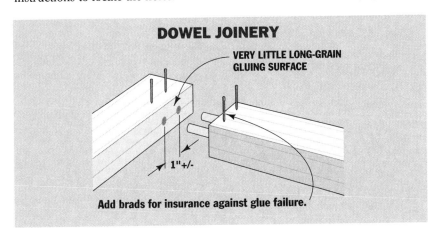

DOWEL JOINERY

VERY LITTLE LONG-GRAIN GLUING SURFACE

1"+/-

Add brads for insurance against glue failure.

Joining Rails and Stiles with Biscuits

Biscuit, or plate, joinery offers an excellent alternative to the conventional mortise and tenon for joining rails and stiles in cabinet doors and for face frames and the like. I've also seen biscuit joints in full-sized leg-and-apron constructions, but I don't think we know enough about the biscuit joint's ultimate strength to rely on it there. I wouldn't rely on biscuits to join an entry door either.

Making a Biscuit Joint

To join corners with biscuits, cut your workpieces and put them in their relative positions on the bench. Mark a centerline across each joint. Most biscuit joiners have a centerline engraved into the baseplate and fence, so you can locate the slots accurately by aligning the center mark on the machine with the mark you drew across the joint.

Always use the largest biscuit you can fit across the width of the

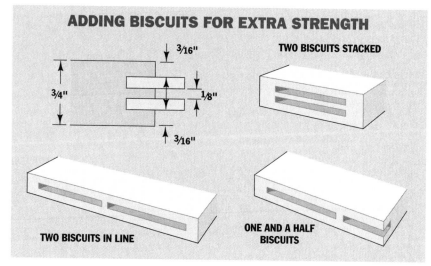

ADDING BISCUITS FOR EXTRA STRENGTH

3/16"

3/4"

1/8"

3/16"

TWO BISCUITS STACKED

TWO BISCUITS IN LINE

ONE AND A HALF BISCUITS

parts. If the edges of the pieces will show, try to allow about 1/8 inch or so at either end of the slot as insurance against the joiner shifting as you cut. If there is room, add another slot beside or underneath the first, as shown in *Adding Biscuits for Extra Strength*. A 3/4-inch piece of wood is thick enough for two biscuits, spaced as shown. In some situations, you may have room for one and a half biscuits. There's nothing wrong with sawing one in half.

Recently, specialty manufacturers have introduced short, wide biscuits specifically for the narrow

rails and stiles of solid wood frame-and-panel constructions, such as cabinet doors. These biscuits, which are much rounder than the standard ones, require a special cutter, but they are worth the extra trouble.

With narrow pieces such as rails and stiles, I find you get a more accurate result if you remove the machine's fence and rest the base of the machine on the bench, plant the workpiece face-side down, and use the fixed distance from the bottom of the machine's base to the blade to determine the slots' location. When you need a different dimen-

SLOTTING NARROW PIECES

CENTER MARK

END BLOCK

Spurs on the biscuit jointer bite into the blocks to hold the machine in place.

Sole of the biscuit joiner rides on the bench top.

TROUBLESHOOTING

ASSEMBLING BISCUIT JOINTS

Always test fit biscuit joints, with a biscuit in each slot, before you glue up. If one slot is somehow not cut to full depth, it will prevent the joint from closing. Rather than recutting the slot, which risks making it uselessly wide, switch to the next smaller-sized biscuit.

sion, put a flat, smooth shim under the baseplate or the workpiece.

To help prevent lateral movement, most biscuit joiners have spring-loaded spurs on either side of the cutter that are supposed to press into the workpiece. With narrow pieces, however, the spurs are often too far apart to catch, so use the jig shown in *Slotting Narrow Pieces*.

Designing Mitered Tenons

In leg-and-apron construction, typical for chairs, stands, and table bases, the mortises intersect inside the leg, as shown in *Typical Leg-and-Apron Constructions*. In order not to interfere with one another, the ends of the tenons are mitered, leaving a gap of about $1/16$ inch.

For the strongest possible connection, you have to divide the amount of available wood as equally as possible between the adjoining pieces. This may mean offsetting the tenon. There are three common situations, as outlined here:

● When the leg is flush with the apron, you can make the inner tenon shoulder the minimum $1/8$ inch wide. Then divide the remaining apron thickness equally between the tenon and the outside cheek, so that each will resist stress equally.

● When the apron is minimally inset, make the inner shoulder the minimum $1/8$ inch wide, and lay out the inner mortise cheek line on the leg. Divide the remaining width of the leg equally between the tenon and the cheek. This permits a thicker tenon than in the first case.

● When the apron is centered on the leg, make the minimum $1/8$-inch shoulder on each side, with the remaining thickness going to the tenon.

Making a Pegged Mortise and Tenon

If you don't trust the holding power of glue, you can peg the joint, as shown in *Pegging a Mortise and Tenon*. This way, if the glue fails, the pegs will hold the joint together. Glue and clamp the

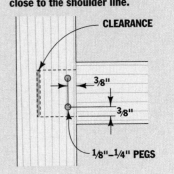

PEGGING A MORTISE AND TENON

Use two pegs per joint, relatively close to the shoulder line.

CLEARANCE

$3/8$"

$3/8$"

$1/8$"–$1/4$" PEGS

joint before you drill for the pegs.

In general, use two pegs, between $1/8$ and $1/4$ inch in diameter, through each joint. Space them as wide apart as you can, out to about $3/8$ inch from the edges of the tenon and about the same distance from the shoulder.

The pegged joint offers opportunities for decoration. You can turn pegs from a contrasting wood, you can turn them with decorative heads, or you can whittle square heads on round pegs.

FACT OR FICTION

SHOULD YOU DRAWBORE?

Drawboring is a timber-framing technique meant for large beams of uncertain moisture content. The basic maneuver is to drill through the mortise cheeks, drill an offset hole through the tenon some distance closer to the shoulder, and then drive a peg home after reassembling the joint. This "draws" the shoulders together.

Drawboring is unnecessary in furniture making, since the joints can be drawn up with clamps. In fact, it may even introduce stress into an otherwise good joint.

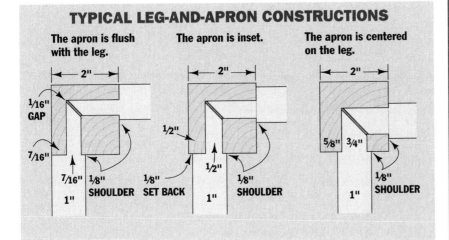

TYPICAL LEG-AND-APRON CONSTRUCTIONS

The apron is flush with the leg.

2"

$1/16$" GAP

$7/16$"

$7/16$" $1/8$"
SHOULDER
1"

The apron is inset.

2"

$1/2$"

$1/8$"
SET BACK

$1/2$"

$1/8$"
SHOULDER
1"

The apron is centered on the leg.

2"

$5/8$" $3/4$"

$1/8$"
SHOULDER
1"

PARING TO A LINE

If you can pare wood cleanly back to a knifed line, you will be able to shape, and fit, virtually any joint. This is a fundamental skill for all woodworkers.

Accurate paring depends upon a sharp bench chisel, as well as on your ability to apply the full strength of your body in a controlled way. There are two basic situations: vertical paring and horizontal paring. Vertical paring allows you to clean up a badly sawn shoulder line in the hardest of hardwoods. Then horizontal paring helps you precisely remove wood down to a layout line.

The photos here show the basic hand grip and stance of each technique. Here are the steps for the two situations:

Vertical Paring

STEP 1 Knife the layout line, and place the wood flat on a cutting board atop the workbench.

STEP 2 Hold the chisel in your fist, with your thumb on the end of the handle. Bend your elbow and press your thumb into your shoulder. Take a marching stance, and bend forward from the waist, as shown below (left), until the tip of the chisel bears upon the workpiece. Grasp the chisel blade in your other hand with the back of your hand on the work and the blade grasped between your thumb and the side of your index finger, as shown below (right).

STEP 3 Drive the chisel downward into the wood by shifting your weight forward and flexing your knees. The power should come from your shoulders and hips, not from your arms and hands. The hand resting on the workpiece guides and controls the cut.

Horizontal Paring

STEP 1 Using either a knife or a marking gauge, mark the line to which you wish to pare on both sides of the workpiece.

STEP 2 Put the work in the bench vise, level and tight. Stand in front of the vise, with your feet in a marching stance, one foot ahead of the other, and your right arm tight to your body, as shown on the opposite page (left). Power for the cut comes from your feet, legs, and hips, not from your arms or shoulders.

STEP 3 Set the butt of the chisel in the palm of your hand, as if

Bend forward from your waist to drive the chisel into the workpiece.

To pare vertically, grasp the chisel in your fist and bring the knuckle of your thumb toward your shoulder.

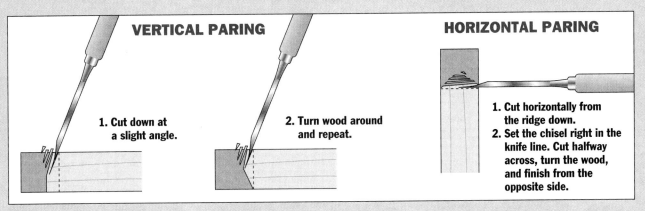

VERTICAL PARING

1. Cut down at a slight angle.

2. Turn wood around and repeat.

HORIZONTAL PARING

1. Cut horizontally from the ridge down.
2. Set the chisel right in the knife line. Cut halfway across, turn the wood, and finish from the opposite side.

it were an extension of your forearm. Set your elbow against your hip.

STEP 4 Grasp the blade of the chisel near the edge, between the thumb and first finger of your other hand. This grip helps you locate the cut. The knuckles of your fingers become a stop and support, allowing you to control the cut, as shown below (right).

STEP 5 Set the blade of the chisel into the wood you want to remove, placing it about halfway up from the marking gauge line. Lower your driving hand so the chisel slopes a few degrees upward. Push from your feet so the blade slices into the wood, removing some of the waste on an upward slope, as shown in *Horizontal Paring*.

STEP 6 Work down to the gauge line in stages, maintainng the upward slope with each cut.

On the last cut, start the chisel right in the gauge line.

STEP 7 Rotate the work in the vise and repeat from the other side, so you end up with a clean ridge of wood in the center of the workpiece.

STEP 8 Set the chisel in the knife line, bring it down toward level, and pare a shaving off of the ridge of wood. Continue paring until the hill is gone and the chisel leaves the wood right on the knife line as it exits on the other side.

STEP 9 Check the result with a combination square. When you set the square on either side of the workpiece, its blade should rest on the original knife line on the other side.

Stance is the key to paring horizontally. The power for the cut comes from your feet. Grip the chisel as if it were an extension of your forearm. Your other hand guides the cut, with your thumb on top of the blade and four fingers below.

Control the cut by trapping the blade between your thumb and index finger, with your knuckles resting on the workpiece.

Making Cross-Halves

The cross-half joint is a lapping joint that makes a crossing intersection, usually of equal-sized parts, as shown in *Cross-Halving*. It's different from the half-lap (described later) in that both of the pieces continue on, past the joint. It's used in stands and small tables and in any other support structure where you want two pieces to make a cross. The intersecting parts can lie flat or stand on edge.

You create the joint by cutting away most of the waste on the table saw, then paring to the layout lines with a sharp chisel. The completed parts should fit together snugly, with no more than very light clamping. If you have to crush the joint together, it's too tight. Follow these steps to make the joint:

STEP 1 Set a marking gauge to half the thickness of the wood, and lay out the bottom of the part you intend to cut. Knife lines to mark the sides of the cutout.

STEP 2 Set the saw to the depth of the joint. Clamp stop blocks onto the miter gauge or crosscut table to mark the ends of the cut, as shown in *Cutting the Recess*.

STEP 3 Cut one side of the joint, then move the work to the other end stop and cut the other side. Break up the waste with a couple of saw cuts in the center.

STEP 4 Set the piece in the vise, and choose a bench chisel that will fit inside the cutout. Remove the waste by paring horizontally.

STEP 5 Glue and clamp the joint together. Spread glue on the end-grain surfaces of the mating parts as well as on the long grain. This will help keep the joint from developing a visible crack as the wood moves.

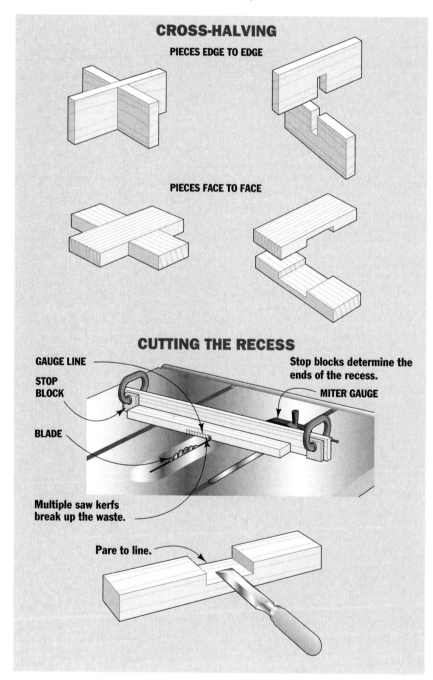

CROSS-HALVING

PIECES EDGE TO EDGE

PIECES FACE TO FACE

CUTTING THE RECESS

GAUGE LINE

STOP BLOCK

BLADE

Stop blocks determine the ends of the recess.

MITER GAUGE

Multiple saw kerfs break up the waste.

Pare to line.

Making Half-Laps

The half-lap, shown in *The Half-Lap*, doesn't seem like much of a joint, but with modern glues, it can be quite serviceable—provided the mating surfaces are flat and that it's clamped up in every direction while the glue sets. The shoulder helps the joint resist stress, which otherwise probably would tear it apart. Ordinarily, the half-lap is best used on work tables and the like, but it can also be decorative if you leave the pieces proud and chamfer the edges.

The pieces are essentially rabbeted. Make the cuts on the table saw, as you would cut a tenon, but with only one shoulder.

The half-lap joint can be used to make a T-shaped construction. Make the housing by sawing the shoulders and paring away the waste, the same as in cross-halving.

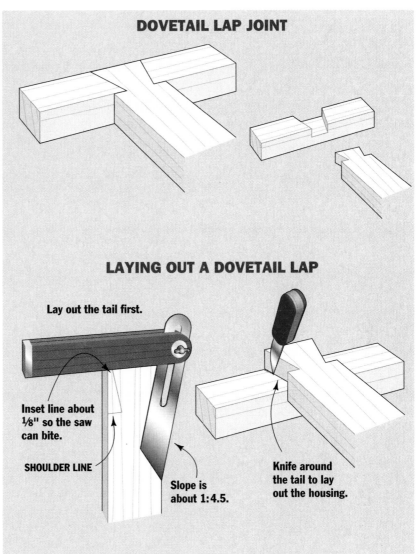

DOVETAIL LAP JOINT

LAYING OUT A DOVETAIL LAP

Lay out the tail first.

Inset line about ⅛" so the saw can bite.

SHOULDER LINE

Slope is about 1:4.5.

Knife around the tail to lay out the housing.

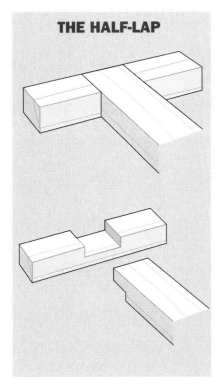

THE HALF-LAP

Making Dovetail Laps

The dovetail lap, as shown in *Dovetail Lap Joint*, is made by cutting one workpiece into a dovetail shape, then housing it in a cutout in the adjoining piece.

To make the dovetail lap joint, cut the tail part first, then scribe around it to lay out and cut the housing, as shown in *Laying Out a Dovetail Lap* and as outlined here. I generally use a slope of 1:4.5 for large dovetails of this type.

STEP 1 Knife the dovetail shoulder line across both edges and across one face of the tail piece.

STEP 2 Scribe a line ⅛ inch from each edge of the piece to mark the widest part of the dovetail.

STEP 3 Draw the slope of the dovetail with a sliding T-bevel.

STEP 4 Cut the shoulders and the face on the table saw.

STEP 5 Saw the dovetail angle with a handsaw or on the band saw.

STEP 6 Set the dovetail in position on the other piece of wood, and draw around it with a sharp knife.

STEP 7 Saw along the layout lines to the proper depth, and chisel out the recess. If you have a set of flat-bottomed Forstner bits, you can establish the depth of the recess by drilling, and you can drill out a lot of the waste.

Making Slip Joints

There are two kinds of slips joints, as shown in *Slip Joints*. When the joint joins one piece to the middle of the other, it is called a bridle joint. The same joint at the ends of both pieces is called an open mortise and tenon. Functionally they are very similar to a regular mortise and tenon and can be as strong.

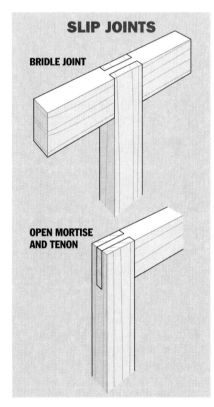

SLIP JOINTS

BRIDLE JOINT

OPEN MORTISE AND TENON

The open mortise and tenon is a good joint for the understructure of workbenches and kitchen islands, and it can also look good connecting the seat rail and arm of a chair. Here's how to make the joint:

STEP 1 Proportion the joint with an equal amount of wood on each piece.

STEP 2 Cut the tenon with the router, on the table saw, or on the band saw.

STEP 3 Cut the two sides of the slot on the table saw with a tenoning jig. This will probably leave a bit of extra wood in between.

STEP 4 Set the piece upright in the vise, and saw out as much waste as you can with a coping saw.

STEP 5 Trim the socket down to the layout lines by horizontal paring, as described in "Paring to a Line" on pages 66–67.

STEP 6 If you're making a bridle joint, cut the notches as described in "Making Cross-Halves" on page 68.

Making Bolted Rail Joints

In utility constructions, such as workbenches, you may decide you want the strength and simplicity of a bolted rail joint. In its simplest form, the joint features a long bolt hole drilled through the leg and into the rail. A D-shaped hole receives the nut and washer, as shown in *A Bolted Connection*. The end of the rail is cut square—there's no wooden interlock.

To avoid having the wood give way, the bolt must penetrate at least 2 inches in hardwood rails and 3 inches in softwood. A $1/4$-inch bolt is usually strong enough.

When the leg shrinks in thickness, you can always tighten the bolt. However, when the leg subsequently swells, the bolt will exert tremendous pressure on the wood in the rail. To prevent failure, it's critical to distribute the stress with large washers on both ends of the bolt. If you stack several washers in graduated sizes, you also create

a nice design detail. Follow these steps to make a bolted rail joint:

STEP 1 Drill the hole in the leg.

STEP 2 Assemble the pieces with clamps and blocks, taking care not to block access to the hole.

STEP 3 Use the hole in the leg as a pilot to drill into the rail end.

STEP 4 Drill the large hole through the rail with a Forstner bit.

STEP 5 Knife a line tangent to the hole, and lay out the top and bottom of the D-shape. Chisel it out.

Making Picture Frame Joints

The traditional corner of a picture frame is a neat miter, as shown in *Mitered Frames*. Most framers first make two L-shapes by joining two adjacent pieces, then they join the subassemblies, completing the frame. Follow the steps here:

STEP 1 Set one piece upright in the vise, with the face of the miter above the surface of the workbench.

STEP 2 Start two finishing nails into the second piece. Drive the nails until their points just come through

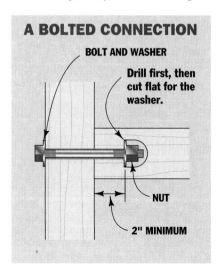

A BOLTED CONNECTION

BOLT AND WASHER

Drill first, then cut flat for the washer.

NUT

2" MINIMUM

the face of the miter. Predrill holes for the nails if splitting is a concern.

STEP 3 Hold the second piece in place on the first and drive the nails. Leave the heads proud until you've joined the subassemblies, in case you have to pull them out for adjustments.

STEP 4 For extra strength, drive a nail or two from the opposite direction.

Biscuit Miters

An alternative to nailing a miter joint is to use biscuits to secure the joint. A picture frame joint doesn't need to be as strong as that in a cabinet door, so a single small biscuit will be enough.

Feathered Miters

A feather is a slip of wood inserted into a saw kerf cut through the assembled parts of a joint. It's a very strong way to reinforce miters, as explained here:

STEP 1 Cut the miters and assemble the frame with glue. Use a strip of rubber cut from an inner tube to clamp it together. The glued miter has no strength, but it will hold long enough for you to saw the kerfs.

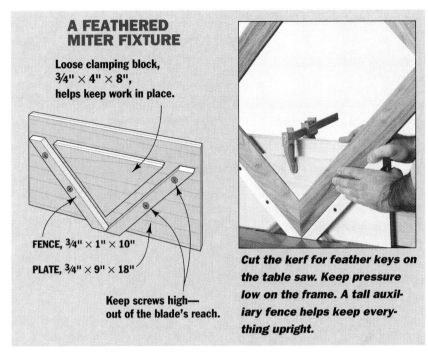

A FEATHERED MITER FIXTURE

Loose clamping block, 3/4" × 4" × 8", helps keep work in place.

FENCE, 3/4" × 1" × 10"

PLATE, 3/4" × 9" × 18"

Keep screws high— out of the blade's reach.

Cut the kerf for feather keys on the table saw. Keep pressure low on the frame. A tall auxiliary fence helps keep everything upright.

STEP 2 Make a table saw fixture to hold the frame, as shown in *A Feathered Miter Fixture*. Basically, it is a cradle for the corner of the frame. Add a tall auxiliary fence to the rip fence to keep it upright while you saw the kerf for the feathers.

STEP 3 Raise the saw blade so the kerf will extend close to, but not through, the inside corner of the frame. Saw all four corners.

STEP 4 Measure the width of the kerf with a dial caliper. Make slips of the same wood or wood of a contrasting color if you prefer. Start by sawing a strip slightly too thick, then bump the fence over and recut until the strip is the precise thickness you need.

STEP 5 Spread glue on the slips and push them into place. Trim them after the glue dries.

Dovetail Keys

A dovetail key looks difficult to make, but it is very similar to making feathered miters, as follows:

STEP 1 Rout the kerf in the frame on the router table with a dovetail bit. Use a jig similar to the one in the photo.

STEP 2 Tilt the blade on the table saw to make a long strip of key stock.

STEP 3 Spread glue on the keys and push them into place. Trim them flush after the glue has dried.

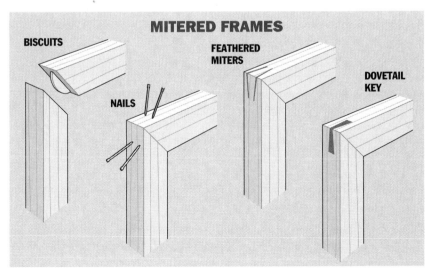

MITERED FRAMES

BISCUITS

NAILS

FEATHERED MITERS

DOVETAIL KEY

Adding Decorative Moldings

It's very common to mold or shape a decorative profile on the inside edges of frames for door panels or furniture parts. However, whenever you profile the edges, you will need to accommodate the molding in the joint. There are three ways of doing this that will result in about the same look.

- Leave the rails and stiles square, and plant the moldings. This means making the moldings as separate pieces and mitering them to fit around the inside edges of the frame. This is the simplest solution, and in most cases, it is also the best. It permits you to use a molding of any complexity.
- Mold the rails and stiles, cut the molding back to a miter in the area of the mortise, and miter the tenon molding to fit. This is called stuck molding, and it is a reasonable small-shop solution.
- Mold the rails and stiles, and cope-cut the tenon shoulders to fit over the profile of the mortise piece. This requires a pair of matched router or shaper cutters and a dead-accurate setup.

A fourth method is to assemble the square frame and then rout a shape around the inside edge. This leaves a characteristic round inside corner instead of a crisp miter. The round corner is mostly end grain, so it usually becomes blotchy under a finish. This rounded edge is commonly seen on quick production cabinets, but to me, it is a poor choice.

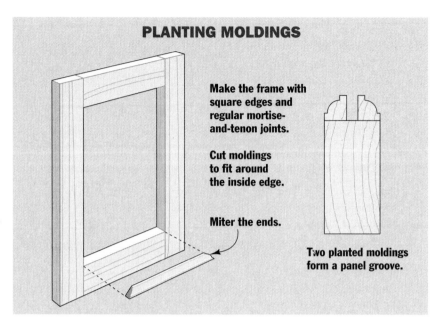

PLANTING MOLDINGS

Make the frame with square edges and regular mortise-and-tenon joints.

Cut moldings to fit around the inside edge.

Miter the ends.

Two planted moldings form a panel groove.

Making Planted Moldings

You can plant moldings of any complexity—including undercut shapes, multiple moldings, and moldings with rabbets that wrap over the frame's edge.

A big advantage of using planted moldings is that you make the frame without any complexities or complications, not even a panel-retaining groove. Join the frame with basic mortise-and-tenon joints, then form the panel groove with the applied moldings, as shown in *Planting Moldings*. To fit the moldings, test fit the frame, then follow these steps:

STEP 1 Miter one end and offer the molding up to the frame.

STEP 2 Mark the miter on the other end and cut it (a chop saw is a real help). Verify the fit.

STEP 3 Tack down the molding, leaving the heads of the brads proud, so you can pull them to adjust the fit.

STEP 4 Proceed to the next length of molding and cut it to fit.

Once everything fits, you can glue the moldings to one another and to the frame. If the panel has to be removable, as is the case with glass, use brads without glue.

Making Stuck Moldings

To fit stuck moldings, you mold a decorative profile directly on the inside edge of a frame, then pare the molding back to a miter in the area of the mortise and cut a matching miter on the tenon piece, as shown in *Fitting Stuck Moldings*. The between-shoulders length of the tenoned piece must be figured from the base of the molding on the mortised piece. Follow these steps:

STEP 1 Make the joints in your usual way, then mold the edges.

STEP 2 Fit the joints together as far as possible. Knife the miters.

STEP 3 Pare the molding on the tenon piece to 45 degrees. Use a chisel block, as shown in *Paring Miters*, for consistency.

STEP 4 Pare the mortised piece. Put a plug of wood into the mouth and chisel into it, as shown. This keeps the mouth of the mortise from tearing out.

FITTING STUCK MOLDINGS

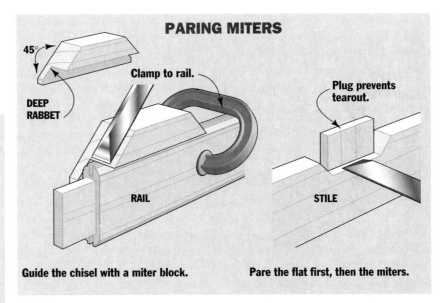

PARING MITERS

45°

DEEP RABBET

Clamp to rail.

RAIL

Guide the chisel with a miter block.

Plug prevents tearout.

STILE

Pare the flat first, then the miters.

Fit pieces together partially to mark for miters.

STILE

RAIL

Lay out miters by extending these points.

Take between-shoulders measurement from here.

The joint has no cosmetic shoulders after mitering.

Making Coped Moldings

In a coped joint, the tenon shoulder is routed to fit over the molding. This reverse cut is called the cope. This joint requires special router bits and is accomplished like this:

STEP 1 Cut the edges of the stiles and rails in your table-mounted router. The fence should be set up tangent to the bit's guide bearing.

STEP 2 Switch to the second bit to make the cope cut on the ends of the rails. Use a sliding fence to push the rails past the cutter. The simplest solution is a 12-inch-square board of ¾-inch particleboard, as shown in *Making the Cope*. Press the assembly firmly against the table and the fence as you cut.

When you have a lot of cabinet doors to make, the coped joint may seem like the ideal solution, and router-cutter manufacturers have promoted it heavily. However, it is just about impossible to achieve consistently good results with the coped joint without industrial equipment, so I don't recommend it.

Instead, use planted moldings, which are just as quick to make. You'll also achieve consistently neat and strong results, and you won't have to invest a lot of money in single-purpose tooling.

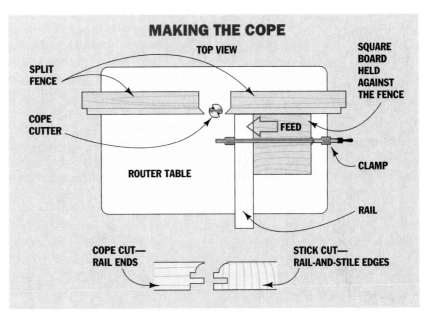

MAKING THE COPE

TOP VIEW

SPLIT FENCE

COPE CUTTER

ROUTER TABLE

SQUARE BOARD HELD AGAINST THE FENCE

FEED

CLAMP

RAIL

COPE CUT— RAIL ENDS

STICK CUT— RAIL-AND-STILE EDGES

Making Haunched Joints

The frame and panel is a fundamental element of furniture construction. It manages wood movement because the solid panel can move in a groove run around the inside edge of a mortised frame. You can use the frame and panel to make cabinet doors and case sides.

You have to make the groove in the rails and stiles before you assemble the frame. The width of the groove usually matches the thickness of the mortise and tenon, though it can be thinner. When you rout the groove, or cut it on the table saw, it's possible to stop it in the middle of the mortises, though many people prefer to carry the groove through to the end of the piece anyway. But when you make the groove with a hand plough plane, there's no way to stop—you have to plough to the end of the mortise piece.

The haunch is a chunk of wood left on the tenon in order to fill the

end of the groove, as shown in *The Haunched Mortise and Tenon*. It has no other purpose, so if you can make a stopped groove, you don't have to make a haunch. Make a haunch as explained here:

STEP 1 Saw the haunch when you saw the faces of the tenon. Make the face and shoulder cuts, as well as those for the cosmetic shoulder, on the inside edge of the tenon, leaving the haunched side alone for now.

STEP 2 Lay out and saw the haunch.

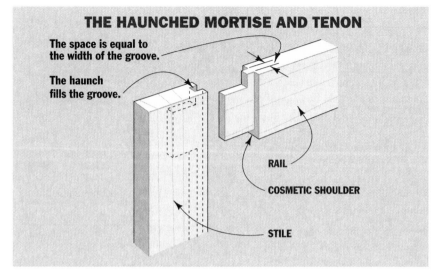

THE HAUNCHED MORTISE AND TENON

The space is equal to the width of the groove.

The haunch fills the groove.

RAIL

COSMETIC SHOULDER

STILE

Making Long-and-Short-Shouldered Joints

You can also set a panel into a frame by rabbeting one side of the rails and stiles. The panel is retained by a molding tacked into the rabbet. The long-and-short-shouldered mortise and tenon fills the rabbet in the area of the joint, as shown in *The Long-and-Short-Shouldered Mortise and Tenon*. To make this joint, follow these steps:

STEP 1 Make the rails and stiles, and cut the mortises in your usual manner. Cut the mortise somewhat deeper than usual, since you'll lose a little of its depth to the rabbet.

STEP 2 Cut the rabbets along the length of the rails and stiles.

STEP 3 Lay out the tenons to fit the mortises. Offset the long shoulder from the short shoulder by a distance equal to the width of the rabbet.

THE LONG-AND-SHORT-SHOULDERED MORTISE AND TENON

RABBET ACCOMMODATES PANEL

Measure shoulder-to-shoulder distance from here.

SHORT SHOULDER

REVERSE VIEW

STEP 4 Cut the tenons to fit, then test fit the joint.

Making Mitered Shoulder Joints

When you want a curved shape between rail and stile, or leg and rail, the curved part should be mitered to the shoulder, as shown in *Rounded Corners*. Otherwise, there'll be a lot of fragile short grain on each of the pieces, which is likely to split if stressed. This situation occurs in such things as chairs, mirror frames, and furniture panels.

The old way to make this joint was to start with workpieces that were wider than required. Then you'd carve away the excess wood. It was a lot of work, and it wasted a lot of wood. I prefer to glue matching blocks of wood to the rail and stile. Then I miter the parts where they meet, before shaping the curve.

Making Angled Mortises and Tenons

Chair seats are usually not square in plan. They tend to be wider at the front than at the back, so the joints between the rails and legs have to be made at an angle. When you mortise the seat rails into the chair legs, you have to make all of the angular adjustment in the tenons and their shoulders, not in the

mortises. This is because it's virtually impossible to make an accurate mortise at an angle to the face of the wood. To make angled mortises and tenons, follow these steps:

STEP 1 Mark out the joints, as shown in *Making an Angled Mortise and Tenon*.

STEP 2 Make the mortise as usual, then cut the tenons on the band saw and pare them to fit.

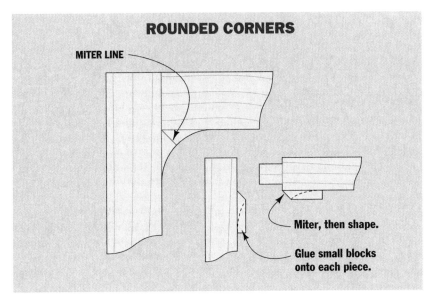

ROUNDED CORNERS

MITER LINE

Miter, then shape.

Glue small blocks onto each piece.

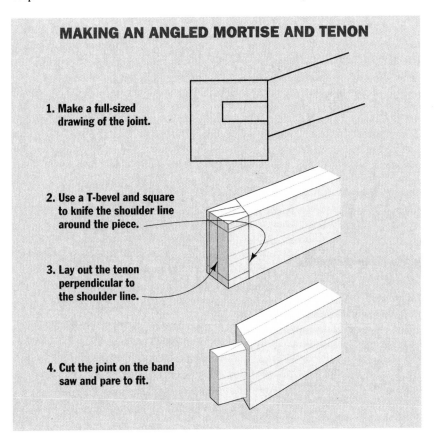

MAKING AN ANGLED MORTISE AND TENON

1. Make a full-sized drawing of the joint.

2. Use a T-bevel and square to knife the shoulder line around the piece.

3. Lay out the tenon perpendicular to the shoulder line.

4. Cut the joint on the band saw and pare to fit.

Making Breadboard Ends

The breadboard end is a cross-grain batten tenoned or tongued onto the end of a tabletop. It's often used on trestle and pedestal-style tables, where the top is not supported by a leg-and-apron understructure. The idea is that the breadboard end will restrain the top from cupping. But in practice, the breadboard is frail, and what really restrains the top is the table understructure.

Visually, the breadboard caps the end grain. However, the breadboard is cross grain to the tabletop and won't move in width as the tabletop does. Consequently, it will always be overhanging the top or short of the edges.

Despite all of this, the breadboard does have its place in some reproduction work. But on a new design, I'd look for a more worthy detail, like the alternative shown in *Adding a Breadboard*. To make a breadboard end:

STEP 1 Divide the thickness of the tabletop into thirds, and rout or saw a tongue on the end.

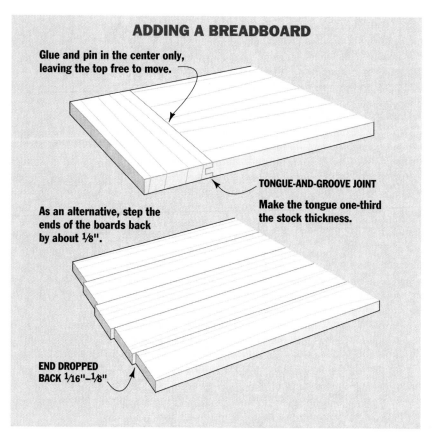

ADDING A BREADBOARD

Glue and pin in the center only, leaving the top free to move.

TONGUE-AND-GROOVE JOINT

Make the tongue one-third the stock thickness.

As an alternative, step the ends of the boards back by about 1/8".

END DROPPED BACK 1/16"–1/8"

STEP 2 Rout a corresponding groove in the batten, as shown.

STEP 3 Spot-glue the batten to the tongue in the center, and peg it there as well, leaving the top free to move in width.

RIPPINGS

VISUAL BREADBOARD

Since the real function of a breadboard end is visual, you can achieve the same visual effect by simply routing a shallow groove across the top of the table, where you think the breadboard end should be. Most people won't detect the difference.

Dividing Wide Tenons

Whenever you find yourself designing a tenon that's more than ten times wider than its thickness, you should divide the tenon, and also the mortise, into two. The division should be roughly into thirds—tenon, space, tenon. The divided mortise is better able to accommodate the stresses of wood movement. This situation arises when making an

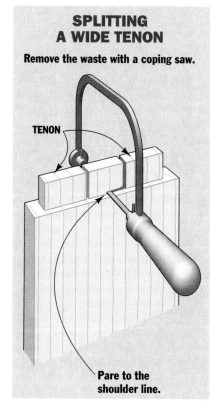

SPLITTING A WIDE TENON

Remove the waste with a coping saw.

TENON

Pare to the shoulder line.

entry door, tenoning the headboard of a bed into the upright posts, or tenoning wide horizontal members into table pedestals to make trestles. Follow these steps to make a divided tenon:

STEP 1 Cut the mortises first.

STEP 2 Make the tenon. Begin by sawing the shoulders as if the tenon were full width.

STEP 3 Saw the faces of the tenons on either the table saw or band saw.

STEP 4 Offer up the tenon to the mortises in order to lay out the division.

STEP 5 Use a coping saw to remove the waste between the tenons, as shown in *Splitting a Wide Tenon*. Stand up the wood vertically in the vise, work the coping saw into the vertical kerf, and saw across. You should be able to saw within 1/16 inch of the shoulder line.

STEP 6 Pare the area between the tenons flat. See "Paring to a Line" on pages 66–67.

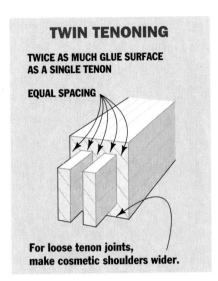

TWIN TENONING

TWICE AS MUCH GLUE SURFACE AS A SINGLE TENON

EQUAL SPACING

For loose tenon joints, make cosmetic shoulders wider.

STEP 1 Lay out the joints.

STEP 2 Make the mortises.

STEP 3 Make all of the face cuts, and saw the tenon shoulders.

STEP 4 Remove the waste between the tenons with the coping saw and bench chisel, on the band saw, or by routing.

As an alternative, you can mortise both parts and use loose tenons. This joint is perfect for loose tenoning.

Making Twin Stub Tenons

Stub tenons join a wide, flat rail to another rail or to a solid carcase side. This situation arises when drawer rails tenon into carcase sides and when the stretcher rail of a table tenons into a cross rail. *Twin Stub Tenoning* shows two typical situations; in each of them, you must be clear about load and grain direction. Your goal is to maximize the long-grain gluing area by dividing the width of the rail into two or more narrow tenons. In some situations where strength is a real issue, you may not want to lose wood to cosmetic shoulders. In these cases, make the tenons the full thickness of the rail.

As always, make the mortises first, then cut the tenons to fit. Remove the waste in between with a coping saw, then pare the shoulder flat.

Making Twin Tenons

When the rail is thicker than 1 inch, as is often the case in chair making, you can greatly increase the strength of the structure by making twin tenons side by side. The total thickness of the two tenons is about the same as if you were to make a single tenon, but the glue area is double. *Twin Tenoning* shows typical proportions; the minimum thickness of each tenon is about 3/16 inch, and the space between should about equal the tenon thickness.

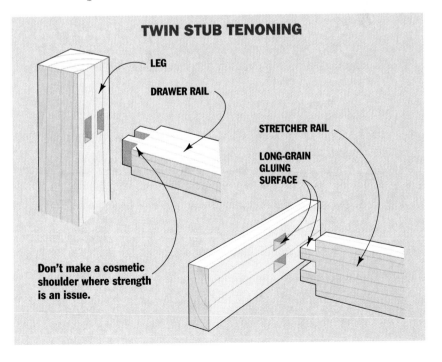

TWIN STUB TENONING

LEG

DRAWER RAIL

STRETCHER RAIL

LONG-GRAIN GLUING SURFACE

Don't make a cosmetic shoulder where strength is an issue.

PUSHING THE LIMITS: The Mitered Showcase Joint

The mitered showcase joint is intriguing because all three pieces are the same. Many woodworkers like to try it for that reason alone.

This elegant showcase joint is a traditional means of joining the frame for a glass-front showcase. While it is quite strong, the joint isn't as robust as a regular mortise and tenon and should be reserved for more delicate assemblies, such as a freestanding curio cabinet or a wall-hung display case.

The key to making this joint is the loose tenon. Making the pieces with traditional, integral tenons is very difficult because one shoulder must be pared to a precise miter around the tenon and the other shoulder must be carefully mortised. However, with loose tenons, mitering the shoulders and mortising the pieces are very straightforward operations, as explained in "Cutting the Showcase Joint."

Note that you'll have to round one end and one side of each tenon to fit it to the mortises. Test fit the joint to figure out which edges to round, then round them with a file.

STEP-BY-STEP: CUTTING THE SHOWCASE JOINT

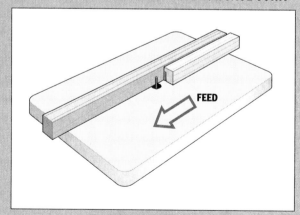

FEED

STEP 1 Make one slot in each piece on the router table. Refer to *The Overall View* for the spacing of the slots.

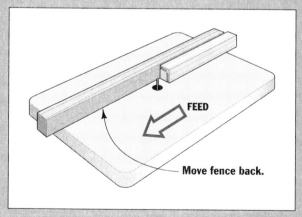

FEED

Move fence back.

STEP 2 Shift the fence to make the second slot in each workpiece. Turn the pieces so the first slot is against the fence.

THE OVERALL VIEW

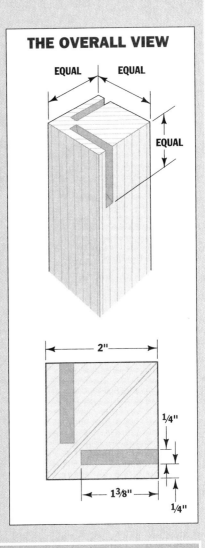

EQUAL EQUAL

EQUAL

2"

1/4"

13/8"

1/4"

Using Tusk Tenons

The tusk tenon extends right through and beyond the mortise, with one or more removable wedges locking the construction together. It's a knock-down joint commonly used in table trestles. Once you understand the technical considerations, it offers many pleasing visual variations, as shown in *Tusk-Tenon Variations*.

The important technical point is the shear stress the locking wedge exerts toward the end of the tusk tenon. The tusk must be large enough to be mortised for the wedge or wedges, and there must be enough wood beyond the wedge to resist its pressure. Then even where there is enough wood, shear failure is likely if the wedge does not bear uniformly against the end grain of the tusk. This means you have to make the mortise slope accurately. The slope should be shallow, an angle of 1:8 or even 1:10, as shown in *Making a Tusk-Tenon Joint*. Set the gradient on your sliding bevel, and check your work as you shape the mortise.

TUSK-TENON VARIATIONS

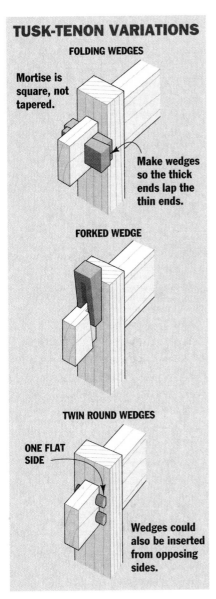

FOLDING WEDGES

Mortise is square, not tapered.

Make wedges so the thick ends lap the thin ends.

FORKED WEDGE

TWIN ROUND WEDGES

ONE FLAT SIDE

Wedges could also be inserted from opposing sides.

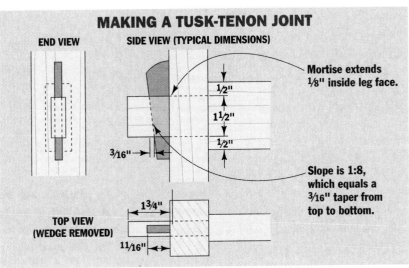

STEP 3 Miter the ends with two cuts on the table saw, guiding the pieces past the blade with the miter gauge set at 45 degrees.

MAKING A TUSK-TENON JOINT

END VIEW

SIDE VIEW (TYPICAL DIMENSIONS)

1/2"

11/2"

1/2"

3/16"

Mortise extends 1/8" inside leg face.

Slope is 1:8, which equals a 3/16" taper from top to bottom.

TOP VIEW (WEDGE REMOVED)

13/4"

11/16"

6
CASE JOINTS: END GRAIN TO FACE GRAIN

Key Ingredients

Case joints connect end grain to face grain in the width of the wood, as shown in *Case Joints*.

The simplest case joints are the butt and the rabbet, which require nails, dowels, biscuits, or some other mechanical reinforcement.

The traditional case joint is the dovetail, which makes its own interlock. Dovetails can be made by hand or machine.

The machine-made equivalent of the dovetail is the box joint—in effect, a square dovetail.

Selection of Stock

The selection of wood for case joinery depends on the size and function of the piece. When you want to make a small box, you're often looking for exotic wood with interesting color and figure, burls, or crotch wood. The wood may distort, but you can manage it because the piece is small.

When you make a large piece with doors and drawers, you must minimize shrinkage and distortion. Although you can't make joints in the disturbed grain that surrounds crotches and knots, disturbed grain is OK in the middle of a panel. While it's possible to use a board distorted with twist or bow, it will

cause you extra problems and extra work, and the result won't be as fine a piece of furniture. You'll have the fewest difficulties if you can choose clean, quarter-sawn wood without knots or other defects.

Solid wood drawers take a lot of time to make and fit, especially if you

cut dovetail joints. It's unwise to use anything but quarter-sawn wood of some mild and stable species, such as maple, ash, or oak. You don't need thick wood to make drawer sides and bottoms. I like to make the sides as thin as I can—3/8 inch is usually enough, and 1/4 inch is often plenty.

People sit on chairs at tables and store their things in boxes and drawers, thus giving you the map of the universe of furniture. You can make chairs and tables with edge joints and rail joints, but to make boxes, you need case joints like the dovetail.

CASE JOINTS

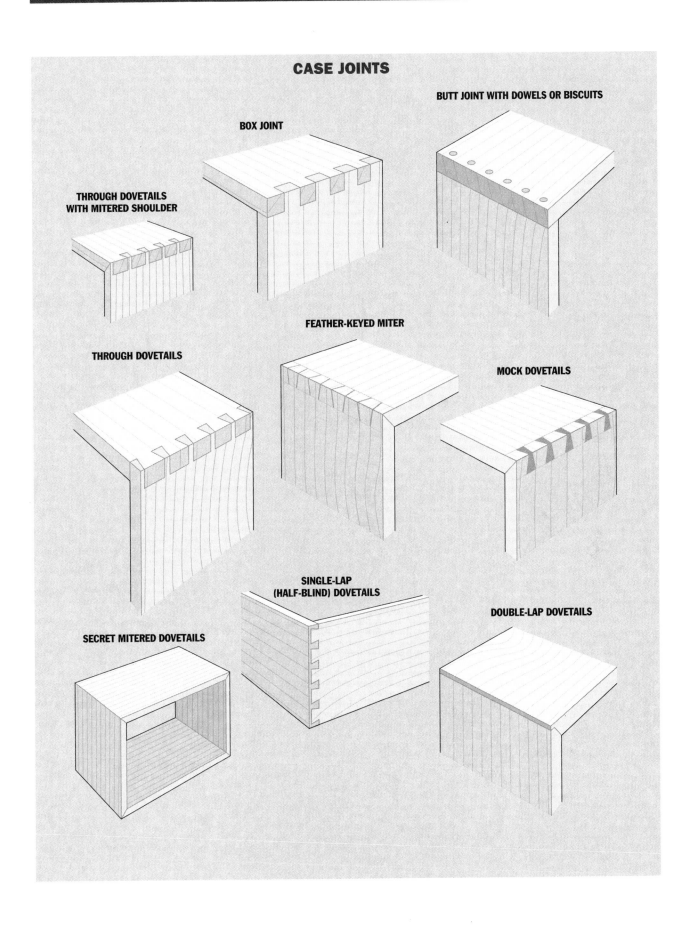

BUTT JOINT WITH DOWELS OR BISCUITS

BOX JOINT

THROUGH DOVETAILS
WITH MITERED SHOULDER

FEATHER-KEYED MITER

THROUGH DOVETAILS

MOCK DOVETAILS

SINGLE-LAP
(HALF-BLIND) DOVETAILS

DOUBLE-LAP DOVETAILS

SECRET MITERED DOVETAILS

Nailed Lap

The nailed lap, or nailed rabbet, is a useful utility joint. It's quick to make and quite strong if you angle the nails, as shown in *Nailing a Rabbet Joint.*

Make the lap ³⁄₁₆ to ¼ inch thick. You can make the lap on the table saw or with a router. The table saw procedure is the same as described for the long-grain rabbet on page 37. Since you'll be holding the pieces on end, long pieces of wood may hit your shop ceiling; in that case, you'll have to rout them.

This is one situation where a hand-held router working against a straightedge is likely to be more accurate than working on the router table. If the board is at all distorted, you can press the router into it better than you can flatten the board onto the table surface. Follow these steps to rout the joint:

STEP 1 Clamp the workpiece to the top of the bench.

STEP 2 Locate the shoulder line of the rabbets, and scribe the lines with a knife or cutting gauge.

STEP 3 Measure the distance from the edge of the router base to the bit's cutting edge, and set a board fence across the workpiece this precise distance from the shoulder line. You can achieve high accuracy by placing a small combination square at the correct measurement and sliding the straightedge up against it. Check the setting at either side of your workpiece, then clamp the straightedge fast.

STEP 4 Using the largest flat-bottomed bit you have, cut the joint. If you have a powerful router, go to full depth in one pass to save time. Otherwise, make multiple passes.

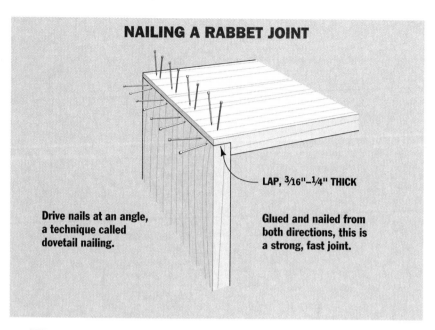

NAILING A RABBET JOINT

Drive nails at an angle, a technique called dovetail nailing.

LAP, ³⁄₁₆"–¼" THICK

Glued and nailed from both directions, this is a strong, fast joint.

When you nail the joint, space the nails as if you were spacing dovetails. Angle the nails about 15 degrees, or the same slope as the side of a dovetail. In hard woods, you may have to predrill holes for the nails. If you use glue and nail the pieces from both directions, you'll have an extremely strong and quick joint.

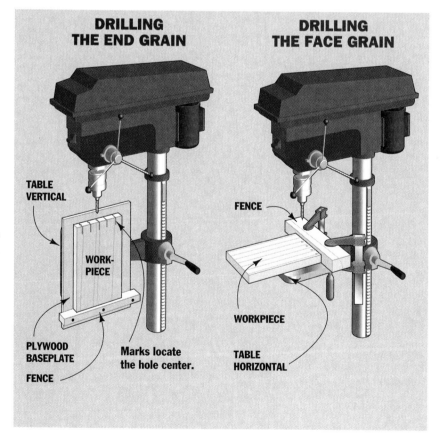

DRILLING THE END GRAIN

TABLE VERTICAL

WORK-PIECE

PLYWOOD BASEPLATE

FENCE

Marks locate the hole center.

DRILLING THE FACE GRAIN

FENCE

WORKPIECE

TABLE HORIZONTAL

Doweled Butt Joint

You can make a successful case joint with dowels. Although it won't be as strong as a dovetail joint, it will work in fairly light-duty situations where you want a clean look. The key is to drill the holes in precisely the right place and to make them truly square to the surfaces.

You can use a manufactured doweling jig in conjunction with a portable drill to keep the holes square and parallel. Square and parallel holes are more important than precisely spaced holes. But I believe the best way to make this joint is with the drill press. Here's how:

STEP 1 Lay out the end grain. Mark the hole centers on the face of the board as well as on the end so you can transfer the marks to the mating piece.

STEP 2 Turn the table on your drill press vertical, and screw a plywood baseplate and fence to it, as shown in *Drilling the End Grain*.

STEP 3 Drill the holes.

STEP 4 Use your square and cutting gauge to transfer the hole locations to the face of the other piece. Punch the hole centers with an awl so the drill bit won't wander.

STEP 5 Drill the holes with the table on your drill press horizontal, as shown in *Drilling the Face Grain*. Clamp a fence to the drill press table to help keep the holes in line.

Short grain can weaken this joint. You can make it stronger by shifting the joint line back from the end of the overhanging piece, creating a "step" between the pieces.

Butt Joint with Biscuits

Biscuit, or plate, joinery allows you to join solid wood or plywood case sides with a butt joint. As shown in *Butt Joint with Biscuits*, you're cutting slots into the end grain of one piece and into the face grain of the other. Keep in mind that the face-grain piece has short grain off one side of the slot, and it is very fragile until the glue sets after assembly. This joint is very quick to make. You can improve the joint in two ways:

- Increase the gluing surface by making a double row of biscuits, which is possible in wood 3/4 inch thick and thicker. Except in very thin wood (less than 1/2 inch), use No. 20 biscuits. Stagger the biscuits as shown.
- Eliminate the fragile short grain by moving the joint back from the overhanging edge. This can enhance the design of many furniture projects.

You can use the fence that comes with the biscuit joiner to locate the slots in the thickness of the wood. However, I find it more accurate to run the sole of the machine on the bench top and to adjust the placement of the slots with shims of plywood. Here's the cutting process:

STEP 1 Lay out the centerlines of the biscuits on both pieces. Mark the top surface of the end grain workpiece as well as its end.

STEP 2 Clamp the end-grain workpiece to the bench. Align the biscuit joiner with the centerlines, and cut the slots in the end grain, with the sole of the machine riding on the bench.

STEP 3 Clamp the face-grain half of the joint flat on the bench, with a fence clamped across it along the joint line.

STEP 4 Transfer your biscuit center marks from the workpiece to the top surface of the fence, and cut the slots with the sole of the machine held vertically against the fence.

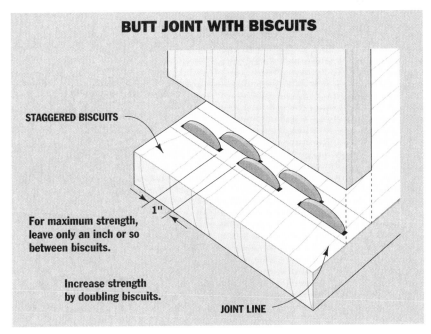

BUTT JOINT WITH BISCUITS

STAGGERED BISCUITS

1"

For maximum strength, leave only an inch or so between biscuits.

Increase strength by doubling biscuits.

JOINT LINE

Box Joint

The box joint (also called the finger or comb joint) can be used in any situation calling for a traditional dovetail. The joint lacks the character of the dovetail, in that all of the lines are straight and square, but it is not without pattern value.

The joint is easy to make on the table saw or router table with the help of the jig shown in *A Simple Box Joint Jig.* Cut both parts of the joint with the same cutter and the same setup, which make the joint look very regular and bold. Scale the width of the fingers to the size of the pieces you are joining—wide fingers look better on larger stock. Thinner fingers mean more glue surface, so the joint is stronger. For most furniture, fingers $\frac{1}{4}$ to $\frac{1}{2}$ inch wide are about right.

Setting Up the Jig

Screw the jig to your miter gauge. With the gauge to the left of

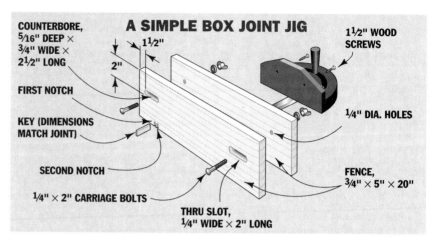

A SIMPLE BOX JOINT JIG

COUNTERBORE, $\frac{5}{16}$" DEEP × $\frac{3}{4}$" WIDE × $2\frac{1}{2}$" LONG

FIRST NOTCH

KEY (DIMENSIONS MATCH JOINT)

SECOND NOTCH

$\frac{1}{4}$" × 2" CARRIAGE BOLTS

$1\frac{1}{2}$"

2"

$1\frac{1}{2}$" WOOD SCREWS

$\frac{1}{4}$" DIA. HOLES

FENCE, $\frac{3}{4}$" × 5" × 20"

THRU SLOT, $\frac{1}{4}$" WIDE × 2" LONG

the cutter, the majority of the jig should extend to the right, as shown in "Cutting Box Joints." Set up a dado blade that is as wide as the fingers you want. If you're working on the router table, use a spiral upcut bit or a straight bit of the appropriate diameter. In either case, set the cutter height to match your stock thickness.

Feed the jig forward, making the first notch in the fence. Shift the front fence over a distance equal to twice the thickness of the kerf. This sets the finger spacing. Make a key

to fit in the first notch. It should match the notch in width and height and stick out about $\frac{3}{4}$ inch in front.

Cut a sample joint and adjust the jig according to how well the joint fits. If the joint is too tight, loosen the wing nuts and move the key toward the cutter. If the joint is loose, move the key away slightly. Keep cutting test joints until you have the jig set up perfectly. Then cut your good stock.

When you assemble the parts, be sure to brush glue onto every mating surface.

STEP-BY-STEP: CUTTING BOX JOINTS

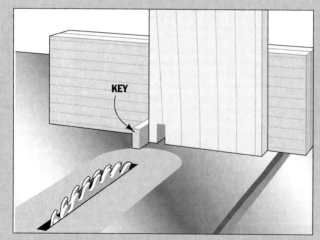

KEY

STEP 1 Butt the first workpiece tight against the jig's key, and cut the first slot.

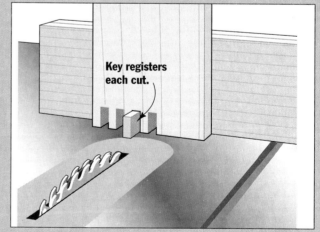

Key registers each cut.

STEP 2 Shift the workpiece so the slot fits over the key, and cut the next slot. Register each successive cut on the key.

Dovetail Basics

The dovetail is the traditional joint for cases and drawers. As shown in *Dovetail Anatomy,* the joint consists of narrow pins, which fit into triangular sockets between wide tails. The pin at the edge of the board is called a half-pin, not because it is half as wide as the others but because it slopes on only one face.

A dovetail increases the amount of glue area between the pieces of wood. The more pins and tails, the more glue interfaces and the stronger the joint will be.

Dovetail Design

The traditional dovetail joint has broad tails and small pins, but the actual layout can vary widely, as shown in *Dovetail Spacing.* In laying out the joint, there are only two design factors to consider:

Dovetail spacing. There's no need to space dovetails uniformly. On a wide joint, they usually vary,

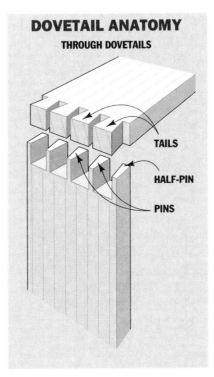

DOVETAIL ANATOMY
THROUGH DOVETAILS

TAILS

HALF-PIN

PINS

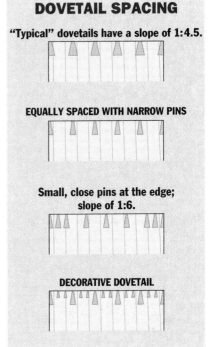

DOVETAIL SPACING

"Typical" dovetails have a slope of 1:4.5.

EQUALLY SPACED WITH NARROW PINS

Small, close pins at the edge; slope of 1:6.

DECORATIVE DOVETAIL

with closer pins and smaller tails near the edges. This has the effect of putting three or four glue lines in the first inch of width, helping to resist cupping.

Dovetail angle. The slope, or gradient, should not vary. I make

dovetails to a slope of 1:4.5. If you make the slope steeper, you begin to approach a box joint; if you make it smaller, it doesn't look as good. Lay out the slope, and set your sliding T-bevel by the method shown in *Setting a Bevel* on page 11.

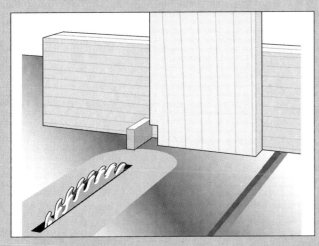

STEP 3 Start the second half of the joint by cutting a notch right at the edge of the second workpiece. Then make the remaining cuts as before.

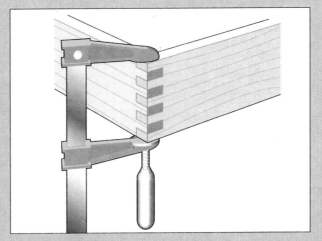

STEP 4 Apply glue to all surfaces, and squeeze the joint closed with bar clamps. Once the joint is tight, apply a single clamp until the glue dries.

Laying Out and Cutting the Tails

Dovetails can be cut by hand or with a router in conjunction with a commercial jig. There are a number of good jigs on the market. Using them is mostly a matter of correctly setting up the equipment, so I won't go into the details here.

Learning to make a through dovetail by hand will show you how the joint works, which will help you get the most out of your router jig. The process is much simpler and faster than people imagine. It uses the skills of laying out, sawing to a line, and chiseling back to a line.

To practice making dovetails, prepare two pieces of $5/8 \times 5^{1/4} \times 18$-inch straight-grained mahogany. Make a joint, see how it fits, and then saw it off and try it again. If you can't get mahogany, look for white pine or poplar. These woods are mild, and they will forgive minor inaccuracies (unlike maple or oak, which hold a grudge). "Making the Tails" shows you the basic procedure, but here are some other points you should keep in mind:

- **Gauging the joint's depth.** When you lay out the joint's baseline, as in **STEP 1**, the line's distance from the end of the board should be $1/64$ inch *less* than the thickness of the wood. This will have the effect of making the ends of the pins and tails recessed slightly below the surfaces of the adjoining boards.

Making the surfaces stand proud of the ends preserves accuracy—you don't have to

shorten the piece to make the joint flush. This allows you to easily make drawers and other boxes to a precise size. As a side benefit, it allows you to glue up the case without bothering about customized clamping blocks.

When you make drawers, perfect fit comes from the way you prepare the wood. First, plane the width of the pins piece so it just enters the height of the drawer opening. Second, mark its length, and crosscut it so it just enters the width of the drawer opening. At the end of the process, when you plane the side of the drawer just down to the end grain of the pins, you're home. It has to fit.

FACT OR FICTION

PINS BEFORE TAILS?

Woodworkers sometimes argue about whether to make the pins first or the tails first. I make the tails and then scribe the pins from them. The joint is easier to lay out this way, plus it is more accurate to saw.

Tails are sawn on an angle into end grain—a cut that is hard to control. However, since this is the first part of the joint, it doesn't matter whether or not it follows the layout line. As long as the saw cut is straight, close is close enough.

Pins are sawn straight down the end grain of the wood. You don't have to worry about sawing at an angle. Because of this, you have maximum control, so it's possible for you to split the layout line and to ensure that the joint will fit.

- **Laying out the tails.** For the strongest possible joint, balance the layout so that in the end, there will be as much wood in the pins as in the tails. Mark all of your lines with a sharp pencil, not with a knife—a pencil line is easier to see. Also, when drawing the slopes, as in **STEP 3**, extend the pencil lines beyond the gauge line—this will help you align the saw.

Note that these layout lines should be drawn on the back of the wood, not onto the face side, because you'll saw with the back side toward you in the vise. The reason for this is that the face side will be the inside of the case, and the back side will be what shows. If you go off in sawing, the error is more likely to be toward the side you can't see than the side you can.

- **Sawing the tails.** Stand the wood upright in the vise to saw and cut down the lines to the baseline, as in **STEP 4**. These saw cuts must be at right angles to the face of the wood, and they must be straight. But it doesn't matter whether you hit the layout line or not. This is one place where close is good enough.

- **Sawing the waste.** When you cut out the waste, as in **STEP 5**, come as close to the knifed line as possible without actually hitting it. The coping saw cuts on the pull stroke, so when you install the blade, the teeth should point toward the handle. Hold the saw in two hands and keep an eye on level.

- **Paring to the line.** Choose a bevel-edged chisel that best fits into the socket and sharpen it.

TRIMMING DOVETAILS

Many woodworkers advocate making the ends of the tails and pins stand proud of the surface, that is, to knife the baseline of the joint $\frac{1}{64}$ inch *deeper* than the thickness of the wood. Their reason is that it is easier to trim the end-grain surfaces flush than it is to plane the side grain. Not only is this false but it also gives up the fundamental accuracy of the wood you so carefully cut to length in the first place.

You'll be cutting into end grain, and only a very sharp chisel will pare cleanly. Pare vertically, first from one side and then from the other, as explained in "Paring to a Line" on pages 66–67. Then pare horizontally right down to the gauge line, but don't undercut it.

- **Sawing the outside shoulders.** Turn the wood on its edge in the vise, and saw off the outside shoulder with your tenon saw. Then use a wide chisel to pare vertically to the gauge line, as in **STEP 6**.

When you've completed the cuts, check your work. Use a small try square to make sure the root of the socket is square to the face of the wood. Poke the square through each socket from one side of the wood, and look at the shoulder line on the other side. The square should touch at that point. Set the square on the other side and look again. You want a flat, square socket, without a hill or a hollow. This completes the tails piece.

STEP-BY-STEP: MAKING THE TAILS

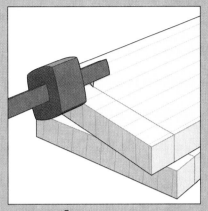

STEP 1 Mark the joint's depth with a cutting gauge. Set the gauge slightly less than the stock thickness.

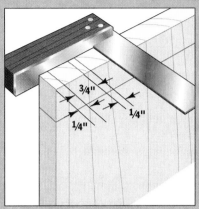

STEP 2 Lay out the tails, making them about $\frac{3}{4}$ inch wide and $\frac{1}{4}$ inch apart.

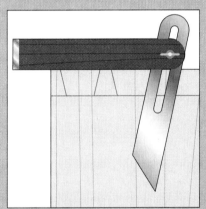

STEP 3 Draw the slopes on the back of the workpiece.

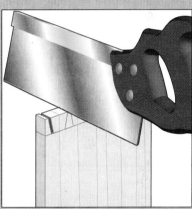

STEP 4 Saw the slopes, keeping straight and square to the wood's face.

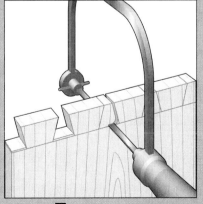

STEP 5 Saw the waste, staying just above the line.

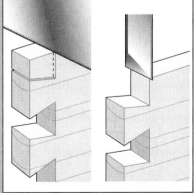

STEP 6 Saw and pare the shoulders dead flat.

Making the Pins

Accurate pin layout is the key to making a tight-fitting dovetail joint. "Making the Pins" shows the steps, but keep these thoughts in mind as well:

- **Scribing the pins.** The pins piece should be vertical in the vise and held so the tail piece sits flat on the bench when it is positioned over the pins piece. Use your square to align the pieces of wood then scribe the tails, as in **STEP 1**

- **Laying out the saw cuts.** Use your square and a sharp pencil to project the corners of the pins past the shoulder line, as in **STEP 2**. These lines will help you saw vertically. Next, pencil an X on the wood you want to remove.

- **Sawing the pins.** Start the kerf at the far side of the end grain, and cut down the waste side of the lines with a tenon saw, as in **STEP 3**. Try to just kiss the knife line. Cut out the waste with a coping saw, and clean up by horizontal paring.

Fitting the Joint

When you have finished paring, stand the pins piece in the vise and set the tails piece in place. Start assembling the joint with hand pressure. Tap the joint home with a light hammer, such as a 10-ounce cross-peen hammer, as shown in the photo. Tap each tail so the joint closes evenly. You won't ding the wood because the movement absorbs the power of the blow.

As you tap, one of three things will occur:

- The joint will be so loose that it drops into place.
- The joint will tap all the way home, meaning it's perfect.
- Some part of the joint will be too tight, so it won't go together.

How can you find tight spots? Listen—the sound the hammer

Listen carefully as you tap the joint together. The sound of a joint that's going together properly is a dull thud. A sharper thwack indicates something is too tight.

makes will tell you where the joint is too tight. If you tap a tail and it moves, the sound will be a dull thud. If the tail is stuck, the sound you hear will be a sharp ring. You'll feel the hammer bounce, and if you per-

STEP-BY-STEP: MAKING THE PINS

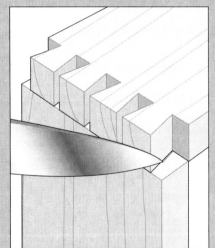

STEP 1 Scribe the pins from the tails.

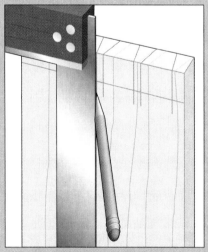

STEP 2 Lay out the saw cuts with a square and a sharp pencil.

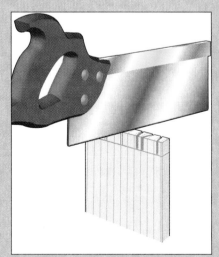

STEP 3 Saw the pins, staying just to the waste side of the line.

sist in tapping that tail, you'll split the wood.

To pare the tight spot, remove the tails piece. If it resists, set a piece of scrap under the joint and tap it upward. Check the faces of the pins and tails for shiny spots and crushed tissue, which indicate where the wood started to bind. Pare down the tight spots with a sharp chisel.

Gluing the Joint

When you make a dovetailed box or drawer, test fit each corner as you make it, but don't assemble all of the pieces until you're ready for glue-up—you may have trouble getting them all apart. There may be quite a few parts to the assembly, so you will have to work quickly. If you can get someone to help you, do so.

Brush a small amount of glue on each mating surface. Start all of the joints with hand pressure, then tap them home with a light hammer and a smooth block of scrap wood. You know they will go, so don't be shy. Hammer all of the joints at least three-quarters of the way home.

Now stand the case on its end, as shown in *Squeezing the Tails*, and with a single bar clamp, work your way along the joints, squeezing each tail down tight. The joint will quickly close up, but be sure you tighten the clamp on each individual tail.

Once all of the joints are closed, check the case for squareness, clamp across the joint to tighten the half-pins, as shown in *The Final Squeeze*, and leave the case alone while the glue dries.

After the joint has dried, you can plane off the surface of the wood until the plane just kisses the end grain of the pins, as shown in the photo. Stop. You're done.

SQUEEZING THE TAILS

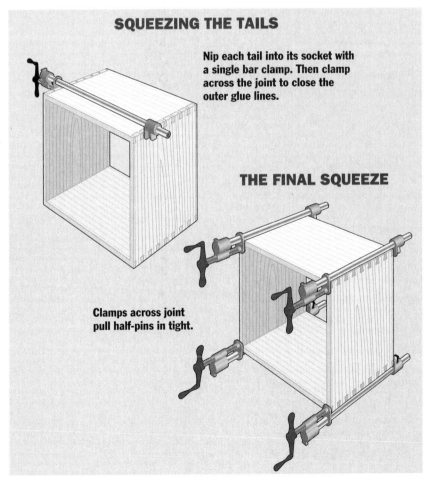

Nip each tail into its socket with a single bar clamp. Then clamp across the joint to close the outer glue lines.

THE FINAL SQUEEZE

Clamps across joint pull half-pins in tight.

Cutting the joint so the tails are proud of the pin ends permits you to smooth-plane the outside of the case after assembly.

Through Dovetail with Mitered Shoulder

You can miter the outside edge of a through dovetail, as shown in the photo (bottom). Normally a dovetail begins and ends with a half-pin, but if you intend to miter it, start with half-tails, as shown in *Mitered Shoulder Dovetail*.

STEP 1 Make the tails piece without the miter, and lay out the pins piece from it.

STEP 2 Lay out the miter on both pieces. Saw the miter on the tails piece, that is, miter the half-tails at the edges. Saw outside the line, then pare right down to it.

STEP 3 Miter the pins piece to fit. Clean up with a sharp chisel.

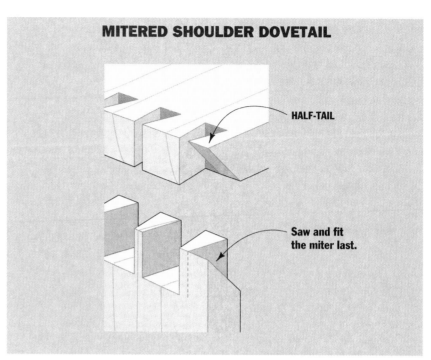

MITERED SHOULDER DOVETAIL

HALF-TAIL

Saw and fit the miter last.

The mitered shoulder (bottom) gives a joint a more finished appearance, as might fit an elegant, wall-hung shadow box. The single-lap dovetail (top) is primarily used in drawer making.

Single-Lap Dovetail

The single-lap, or half-blind, dovetail is the classic drawer joint, and in fact, it is rarely used anywhere else. As shown in the photo (top), the drawer front is usually made of thicker stock than the sides and back, and it's often made of a showier species. The tail pieces are the drawer sides; the pins are cut in the drawer front and back.

You can achieve the effect of a single-lap dovetail if you make a through-dovetailed drawer box and attach a separate drawer front to it. The drawer front can be made of an expensive exotic wood or of a wood you can't readily dovetail, like burl walnut. "Cutting Single-Lap Dovetails" shows the sequence. Keep these additional points in mind as you make the joint:

● **Laying out the joint.** The lap, that is, the piece of wood that hides the ends of the tails, shouldn't be less than 3/16 inch thick, or it may not stand up to the process of cutting and fitting the joint. Determine this dimension, then subtract it from the thickness of the front to determine the length of the tails and to set the cutting gauge. Gauge the length of the tails onto the end grain of the drawer front, and gauge the same distance around the end of the tails piece, as in **STEP 1**.

● **Making the tails.** The layout and cutting processes are the same as you use to make through dovetails. (See "Making the Tails" on page 87.)

● **Laying out the pins.** Set the drawer front in the vise and the tail piece on top, as in **STEP 2** Scribe the shape of the pins through the tail sockets, then square the layout lines down the inside face of the drawer front.

● **Sawing the pins.** Start the saw at the corner of the cut, and sight along the knife lines. Saw down the vertical line without sawing across the end grain, then raise the handle of the saw to cut across the end grain as far as possible without cutting into the lap, as in **STEP 3**.

● **Roughing out the pins.** With the drawer front flat on the bench, set a chisel into the waste about halfway between the baseline and the end of the wood. Tap the chisel into

the wood with a mallet, about half the depth of the socket or as deep as it will readily go. Make this initial cut across all of the pins.

Stand the wood in the vise, and tap the chisel lightly into the end grain to pop out a chunk of the waste. Repeat, working toward the lap line in bites of ¹/₁₆ inch or so, until you establish the depth of the socket, as in **STEP 4**. Lay the

wood flat on the bench, and chisel and rough out the cavity.

● **Paring the pins.** With the wood standing in the vise, use a ¼-inch skew chisel to complete the pins, as in **STEP 5**. You can grind your own skews from ordinary ¼-inch bevel-edged bench chisels. Don't undercut the socket. Cut the remainder of the pin wall with a ¾- or 1-inch chisel. Clean up by vertical and horizontal paring. Tap the joint home.

STEP-BY-STEP: CUTTING SINGLE-LAP DOVETAILS

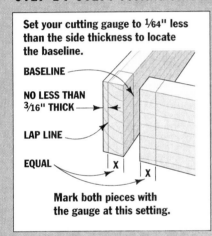

Set your cutting gauge to ¹/₆₄" less than the side thickness to locate the baseline.

BASELINE

NO LESS THAN ³/₁₆" THICK

LAP LINE

EQUAL

X | X

Mark both pieces with the gauge at this setting.

STEP 1 Use a cutting gauge to knife the baseline and the lap line.

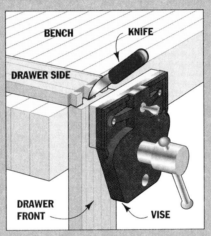

BENCH KNIFE

DRAWER SIDE

DRAWER FRONT VISE

STEP 2 Cut the tails as usual, then scribe the tails onto the drawer front.

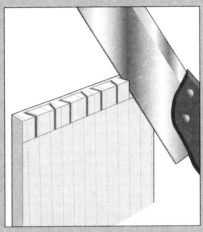

STEP 3 Saw the pins with the saw at an angle. First cut down the board's face, then across the end.

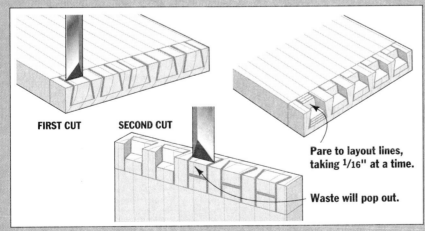

FIRST CUT SECOND CUT

Pare to layout lines, taking ¹/₁₆" at a time.

Waste will pop out.

STEP 4 Rough out the pins by chopping first into the face of the board, then popping out the chip from the front.

A skew chisel reaches into the corners.

STEP 5 Pare the sockets back to the layout lines with a skew chisel.

Double-Lap Dovetail

This joint is hidden—all that shows is a narrow lap of end grain on one surface, as shown in *Double-Lap Dovetail.* Use this joint to make an elegant case, where you don't want a visible joint to interfere with the rest of the design. The edges of the joint can be mitered, and the end of the lap may be beaded.

The tail piece, which you make first, has a narrow rabbet, as shown. After you've cut the rabbet, lay out the tails. Then saw into the waste and chisel the sockets. You may need a hook-shaped marking knife to transfer the shape of the tail sockets to the pin piece. Make the pin piece in exactly the same way you would for a single-lap dovetail. See "Single-Lap Dovetails" on pages 90–91.

Secret Mitered Dovetail

This joint, shown in *Secret Mitered Dovetail,* is tough to cut and rarely used. But it offers the great strength of the dovetail coupled with the elegant simplicity of the miter. You might find use for it in a piece of exacting cabinetry, where even the slight rabbet of the double-lap dovetail would interupt the piece's lines. You might also cut the joint for sheer bragging rights. If that's the reason, don't glue it up, or you won't be able to prove what you've accomplished.

Make the joint in reverse order, that is, pins before tails. If you try to make it in the usual way—tails before pins—you'll find that you can't get into the tails to lay out the pins.

The first step in making the secret mitered dovetail is to lay out and cut a rabbet in both pieces of wood, as shown. Then lay out and cut the pins. Scribe the tails from the pin and chop out the sockets. Close the joint by mitering the overhanging rabbets with a shoulder plane.

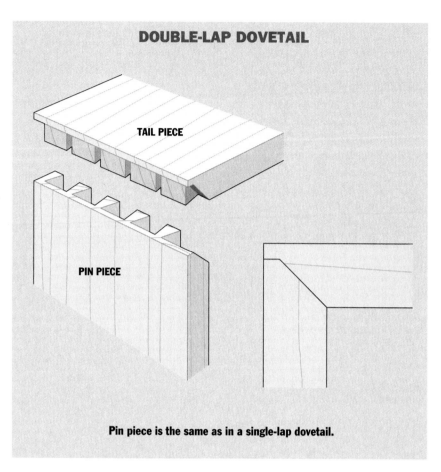

DOUBLE-LAP DOVETAIL

TAIL PIECE

PIN PIECE

Pin piece is the same as in a single-lap dovetail.

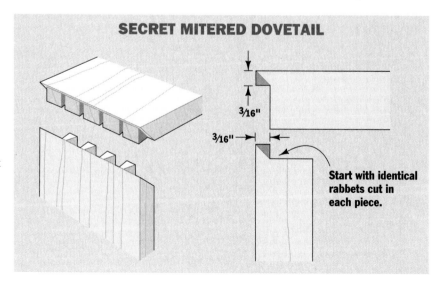

SECRET MITERED DOVETAIL

3/16"

3/16"

Start with identical rabbets cut in each piece.

DOVETAIL JIGS

There are numerous router dovetail jigs on the market today, as shown in the photo. Once set up, they are all capable of fast and accurate work, but within limits.

- When you set up the jig, don't offset the root of the joint as you would when dovetailing by hand. Set it up so the parts fit as flush and as accurate as you can manage. You can't fuss with it afterward, so you have to achieve accuracy in the initial setup.
- Jigs really excel when you can make a lot of parts with the same setup. However, changing the setup is a long-winded process, so jigs are not so good when you are making only one case or box.
- Some jigs do not permit you to adjust the spacing of the pins and tails. To make the joint work out, you have to size the parts to whatever spacing the jig can accommodate. To figure out what increments your jig uses, dovetail a wide board. Then measure the distance from the edge to the centers of the pins across the board. This will give you the widths of the pieces you can dovetail while leaving a half-pin at either edge.
- The slope of the pins and tails is built into the router bit. You can't vary it. What's more, most jigs only work with a specific bit or set of bits. Make sure you know which bits work with your jig before purchasing extras.
- With any of the adjustable jigs, the smallest pins you can make are determined by the diameter of the bit you're using.

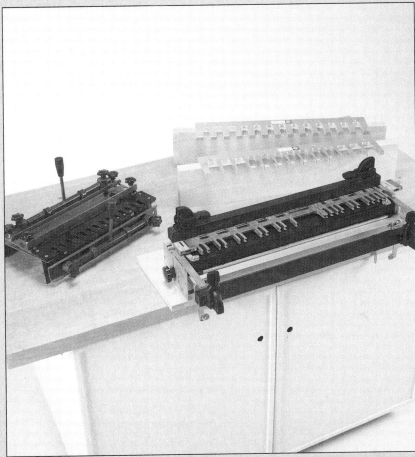

Dovetail jigs range in price from about $50 to more than $400; the more expensive, the more complex and versatile. These jigs are all capable of repeatedly accurate work.

- When using one of the simple half-blind jigs, make sure the bit is clear of the template before picking up the router. If you rout the template, you'll ruin it. For some reason, the guy at the local tool service center has the template part number memorized.
- With the basic half-blind jigs, you adjust the fit of the joint by raising or lowering the depth of cut. (Raising the bit makes the joint looser.) There is essentially one correct setting. Once you get your router set up, you can just leave it that way, provided you are always cutting the same species of wood. But if you work in many species of varying hardness, you'll find that within that "one" correct setting, there is some room for adjustment. Harder woods like maple and oak tend to need a looser fit than soft woods like butternut and alder. The difference is very subtle—no more than a few thousandths of an inch—but it is real.
- Any dovetail jig will yield the best results if you use sharp bits. Dull bits leave a glazed surface that won't glue well and looks terrible.

Housings

Frequently you need to put a shelf or divider in a case. The most common solution is to rout a housing, or dado, the width of which matches the thickness of the wood, as shown in *Housings*. A good fit, plus glue, will hold the shelf in place, even though there is no long-grain gluing surface. Make the housing about ⅛ inch deep in solid wood and ¼ inch deep in plywood, medium-density fiberboard (MDF), and particleboard.

It's common to run the housing right through the front edge of the case side, but it always looks crude. It is better to make a shoulder at the edges of the divider and to cut a shorter housing, as shown in the photo. Make the housing with a plunge router, guided by a fence clamped to the workpiece. You want a little play from end to end, so you can be sure the front edge of the divider is flush with the edge of the case side.

You can also make the shoulder on all four sides of the divider, with a correspondingly narrower housing. The full shoulder adds stability to the case and shows you

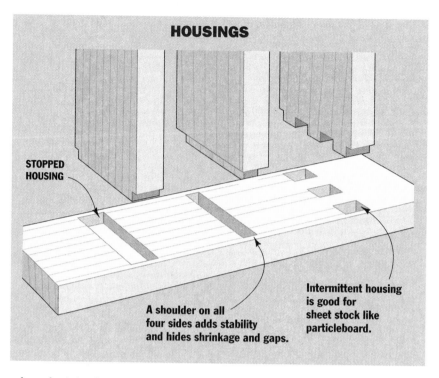

HOUSINGS

STOPPED HOUSING

A shoulder on all four sides adds stability and hides shrinkage and gaps.

Intermittent housing is good for sheet stock like particleboard.

when the joint has seated during clamping.

In MDF and particleboard, the construction will be stronger if you make the tongue and the housing intermittent because man-made sheet materials derive much of their integrity from their surface layers. When you cut right through the surface layer, you create weakness in the piece.

It's important to know that a housed joint has no real strength,

and it will not help suck in the sides of a large case if they're warped. All it does is locate and support a divider and add racking resistance to the case. When you need to install a divider in a more structural role, you should use twin tenons.

Twin Tenons

When you need to use a shelf or divider to pull in the sides of a case, make twin tenons on both edges of the divider, as shown in *Twin Tenons*. The tenons can go through and be wedged on the other side, or they can be stopped. In either case, you'll get plenty of useful long-grain gluing surface on both faces of each tenon.

Make the tenons the full thickness of the wood. You don't really need shoulders, so it's better to avoid the unnecessary work. Two tenons on each side of the divider

The stopped housing (right) gives a case a more finished look.

will be ample in pieces narrower than 6 inches. If the wood is much wider than that, make a third pair of tenons in the middle of the joint. You can ensure that there are no gaps between the divider and the adjoining board by leaving a ⅛-inch tongue in between the pairs of tenons, as shown. Rout a matching housing for the tongue in the adjoining board.

Make the mortises in the case sides before you cut the tenons. If you're making through mortises, lay them out on both sides of the wood, and drill out the bulk of the waste before you square up with a bench chisel. If you're making blind mortises, lay them out on the inside surface, and drill out the waste with a flat-bottomed Forstner bit.

You can saw the tenons by hand, on the band saw, or on the table saw. Lay out the tenons by marking directly from the mortises. If you are working with hand tools, remove the bulk of the waste with a coping saw and then pare.

FACT OR FICTION

ARE SLIDING DOVETAILS BETTER THAN TENONS?

The sliding dovetail is often specified for holding shelves and dividers in place. However, it's an extremely difficult joint to make and fit, and it offers no advantage over a twin tenon. There's no useful gluing surface in the joint—all of its strength comes from the mechanical interlock of the dovetail itself. Yet the joint must be glued, or normal wood movement is liable to work the two pieces apart. The joint must fit very tight if it is to work at all. Consequently, should it swell from being wet with glue, it may seize before it's fully seated. At that point, no amount of clamping or hammering will save the situation—the whole job may be ruined.

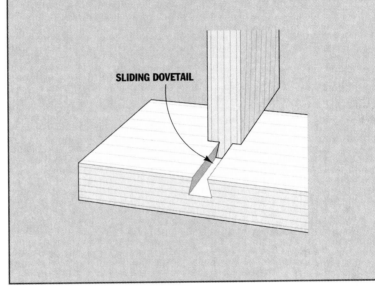

SLIDING DOVETAIL

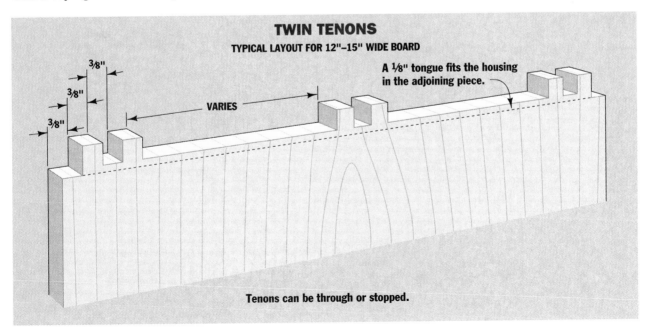

TWIN TENONS
TYPICAL LAYOUT FOR 12"–15" WIDE BOARD

3/8"

3/8"

3/8"

VARIES

A ⅛" tongue fits the housing in the adjoining piece.

Tenons can be through or stopped.

Mitering Case Corners

The splined miter is a workable case joint, although it's not nearly as strong as the dovetail or the box joint. In solid wood, the spline is cross grain to the case sides, but you can control any potential movement problems by cutting the spline into 3-inch sections. (Leave a small gap in between the sections when you glue up.) In plywood and MDF, the spline miter is an excellent joint, provided you don't weaken the case sides by making the slot too deep.

Whatever material the case is made from, the spline should be located right at the root of the miter, as shown in *Splined Miter*.

This way, the slot can be as deep as possible without weakening the case sides. The feather of wood where the slot enters the miter is no more vulnerable to damage than the feather of wood at the tip of the miter, so don't worry about it.

It's tempting to avoid cross-grain problems by sawing the spline out of thin plywood, but this is a mistake. The glues in plywood have little shear strength, as you can demonstrate for yourself: Make a spline-sized strip, and see how easy it is to peel the layers apart. They'll come apart just as easily inside the joint.

Make the miter on the table saw, with the blade heeled over to 45 degrees. You need a sliding crosscut table, and it's best to

clamp the wood to it. There's considerable sideways stress during this cut, and the board will tend to wander if you skip the clamps. Cut the spline grooves on the table saw as well, in the same way I described cutting them for long-grain miters. (See *Cutting Spline Grooves* on page 39.)

When you're ready to glue up, add glue blocks to either side of the joint, as shown in *Clamping a Miter* on page 38.

Miter with Biscuits

When you reinforce a miter with biscuits, the biscuit joiner's fence determines

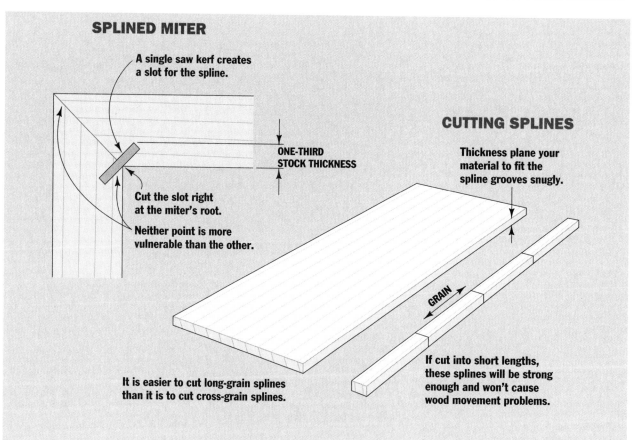

SPLINED MITER

A single saw kerf creates a slot for the spline.

ONE-THIRD STOCK THICKNESS

Cut the slot right at the miter's root.

Neither point is more vulnerable than the other.

It is easier to cut long-grain splines than it is to cut cross-grain splines.

CUTTING SPLINES

Thickness plane your material to fit the spline grooves snugly.

GRAIN

If cut into short lengths, these splines will be strong enough and won't cause wood movement problems.

where the slots land. However, since the slots are intermittent, there's no continuous line of weakness, so you don't have to worry that the slots are not right at the miter's root. Glue up the joint in the same way as for the splined miter, using 45-degree clamping blocks. (For more details, see page 38.)

Feather-Keyed Miter

A feather key is a thin slip of wood glued into a saw kerf. A series of feather keys through a miter will hold the joint together as if it were sewn.

Glue the joint together first, using angled glue blocks. While glue alone doesn't make a very strong miter joint, it will hold the pieces together while you work on them. Just treat the assembly gently. After the glue dries, cut kerfs across the joint for the keys. As shown in *Cutting the Key Slots*, one of the easiest ways to cut the slots is with a tenon saw. A tenon saw will make a kerf the thickness of a veneer. You can make the saw cuts at an angle, which can suggest dovetails, or you can make them square across. Glue slips of veneer in the kerfs, with the grain running perpendicular to the face of the miters.

You can cut the key slots on the table saw as well. Make a jig

that will cradle the assembled parts and guide them against the rip fence, as shown in the photo on page 71.

Mock Fingers, Mock Dovetails

You can also make the feather keys in a dovetail shape, as shown in the photo. Cut the slots with a dovetail bit in a table-mounted router. Guide the pieces along the fence in a cradle jig. (See the photo on page 71.) The depth of the slots should be about half that of the miter. Cut the keys by tilting the blade on the table saw.

CUTTING THE KEY SLOTS

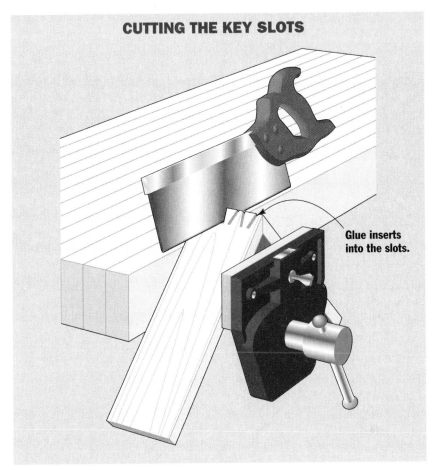

Glue inserts into the slots.

Mock dovetails are actually dovetail-shaped keys inserted into slots cut across a miter joint. Use a contrasting wood for an added visual effect.

Problem Solving
Dovetails

You can patch most dovetail errors. However, you have to judge when it would be better to discard the piece and make another.

PROBLEM	SOLUTION
My dovetails fit pretty well, but there are usually one or two small gaps.	Rather than trying to fill the gaps with slivers of wood, cut along the offending joint line with your saw to create an even gap, then glue a slice of veneer in place for an invisible patch.
I'd like to try to cut very fine dovetails, where the pins come to a point on the narrow end, but my dovetail saw is too coarse to make such a fine cut between the tails.	Try making the cuts with a Japanese *dozuki* saw. This saw leaves a kerf less than half the width of its western counterpart.
My dovetail saw is getting dull, but the teeth are so fine, I don't think I can sharpen them.	Most professional saw shops will sharpen handsaws as fine as 18 teeth per inch for less than $10. Even if you can sharpen your own saws, it's worth having them professionally sharpened every so often to keep them in tip-top condition.
When I set up to rout dovetails with my half-lap dovetail jig, I have real trouble getting the bit set to just the right depth of cut.	First, you have to understand what changing the depth of cut does for the fit of the joint. Raising the bit makes the joint looser, while lowering it makes the joint tighter. (If you lower the bit too much, you'll make your jig lighter by cutting into it.) Once you know what you're after, make adjustments in very small increments until you get the fit you want. If you do a lot of dovetailing, consider buying a router specifically for the job and leaving it set up.
Using my half-lap dovetail jig, I routed a set of dovetails in poplar to test the setup. The joint went together perfectly. But when I routed the joint in the oak I was using for my project, the joint was too tight. What happened?	The initial setup was probably on the tight side. Since poplar is a fairly soft wood, it gave slightly as you pushed the joint home. Oak is more unforgiving. In situations like this, you get better results when you make your test cuts in the same species of wood you're actually using. This practice may cost a little extra, but it is cheap insurance against miscutting a project's worth of lumber.

PROJECTS

SIDE TABLE

Quarter-sawn oak and clean, simple lines give this small table a timeless quality reminiscent of both Shaker and Arts and Crafts furniture.

Despite its diminutive size, this small table offers a wealth of opportunity to practice the joinery presented earlier in this book. Its construction is very traditional—mortises and tenons join the aprons and stretchers to the legs, dovetails join the drawer corners, and slips hold the drawer bottom in place. (Those mortises and tenons joining the center stretchers to the cross rails are through and wedged.) By the time you're finished, you will have gained a good understanding of the way fine furniture is traditionally made—without drywall screws, staple guns, and other expedient measures.

SIDE VIEW

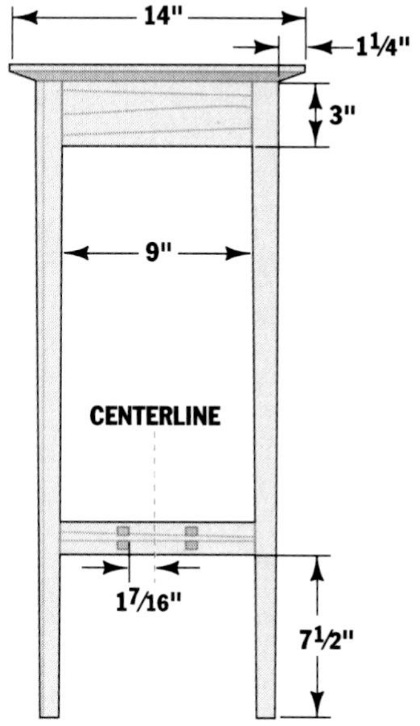
14"
1 1/4"
3"
9"
CENTERLINE
1 7/16"
7 1/2"

FRONT VIEW

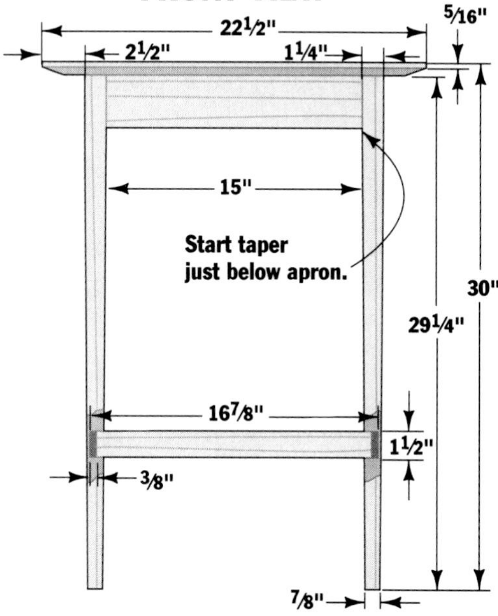
22 1/2"
2 1/2"
1 1/4"
5/16"
15"
Start taper just below apron.
30"
29 1/4"
16 7/8"
1 1/2"
3/8"
7/8"

EXPLODED VIEW

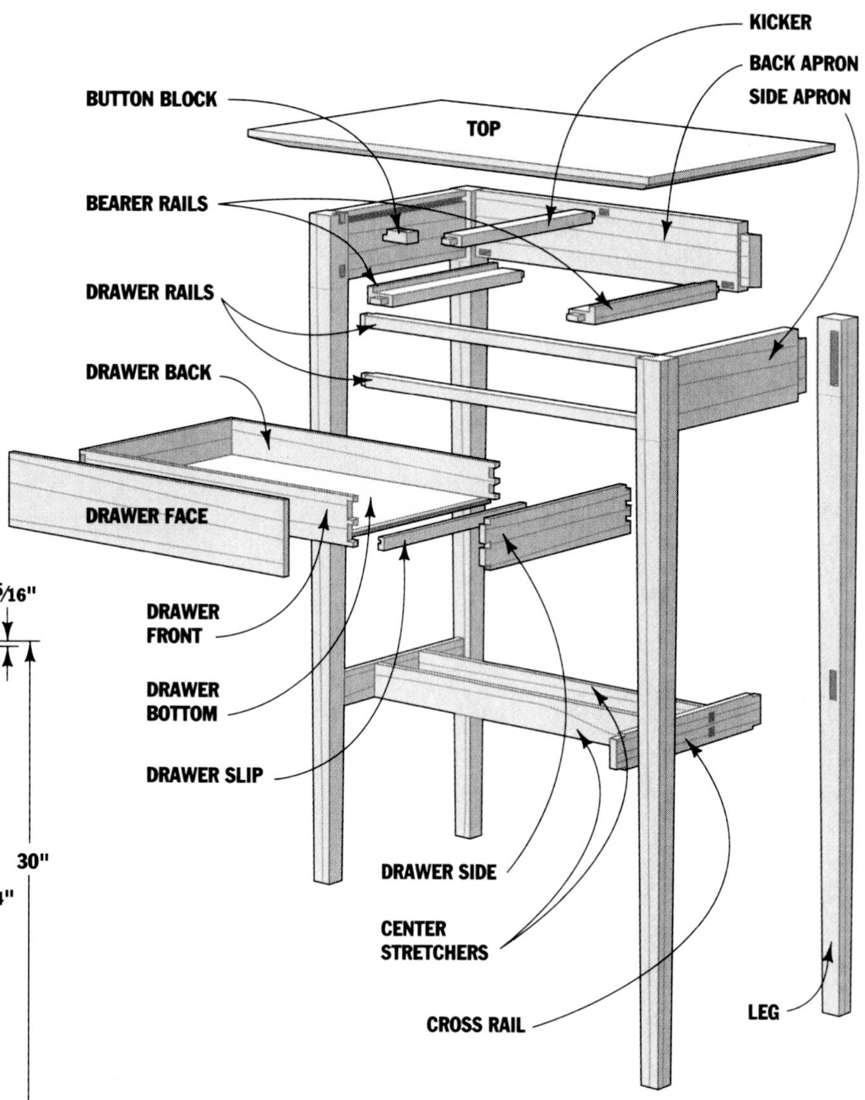
KICKER
BACK APRON
SIDE APRON
BUTTON BLOCK
TOP
BEARER RAILS
DRAWER RAILS
DRAWER BACK
DRAWER FACE
DRAWER FRONT
DRAWER BOTTOM
DRAWER SLIP
DRAWER SIDE
CENTER STRETCHERS
CROSS RAIL
LEG

MATERIALS LIST

PART	QTY.	DIMENSIONS
Top	1	3/4" × 14" × 22 1/2"
Legs	4	1 1/4" × 1 1/4" × 29 1/4"
Drawer rails	2	1/2" × 3/4" × 15 3/4"
Side aprons	2	3/4" × 3" × 10 3/4"
Back apron	1	3/4" × 3" × 16 3/4"
Bearer rails	2	3/4" × 1 7/16" × 10 5/16"
Kicker	1	1/2" × 1" × 10 5/16"
Cross rails	2	3/8" × 1 1/2" × 10 13/16"
Center stretchers	2	3/8" × 1 1/2" × 16 7/8"
Drawer sides	2	5/16" × 2" × 9 3/4"

PART	QTY.	DIMENSIONS
Drawer front	1	5/16" × 2" × 15"
Drawer back	1	5/16" × 1 1/2" × 15"
Drawer slips	2	5/16" × 1/2" × 9 7/16"
Drawer bottom	1	1/4" × 9 9/16" × 14"
Drawer face	1	5/16" × 3" × 15"
Button blocks	4	1/2" × 3/4" × 1 1/2"

HARDWARE

3/4" × #6 flat-head brass wood screws	4	
Brass pull	1	

Procedure

1 Cut the parts to size. Select your stock, and cut the pieces except for the drawer parts and button blocks to the sizes in the Materials List on page 101. You'll probably have to edge glue several narrower boards to make up the top. Cut two of the leg blanks about an inch too long to allow for a horn on the mortised end. (The other two legs have to be cut to exact length to allow for the drawer rail joints.) Leave the cross rails about 2 inches or so too long; you'll trim them to fit later.

Wait until after the table is together to cut the parts for the drawer. Cut stock for the button blocks to the proper width and thickness, but leave it about 9 inches long for now.

2 Cut the leg joinery. Join the upper drawer rail to the legs with dovetail joints and to the lower rail with stub mortises and tenons, as shown in *Leg Joinery Detail.* Join the side and back aprons to the legs with regular mortises and tenons, mitering the ends of the tenons where they meet inside the legs.

3 Add the bearer rails and kicker. Rabbet the bearer rails, as shown in *Bearer Rail Section.* Join the bearer rails and the kicker to the drawer rails and back apron with mortise-and-tenon joints, as shown in *Kicker and Rail Detail.* The bearer rails are notched to fit around the back legs.

4 Taper the legs. Taper the legs on their two inside surfaces, as shown in the *Front View* on page 101 and the

LEG JOINERY DETAIL

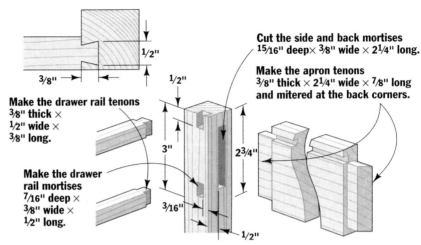

Make the drawer rail tenons ³⁄₈" thick × ¹⁄₂" wide × ³⁄₈" long.

Make the drawer rail mortises ⁷⁄₁₆" deep × ³⁄₈" wide × ¹⁄₂" long.

Cut the side and back mortises ¹⁵⁄₁₆" deep × ³⁄₈" wide × 2¹⁄₄" long.

Make the apron tenons ³⁄₈" thick × 2¹⁄₄" wide × ⁷⁄₈" long and mitered at the back corners.

³⁄₈"   ¹⁄₂"   ¹⁄₂"   3"   2³⁄₄"   ³⁄₁₆"   ¹⁄₂"

BEARER RAIL SECTION

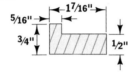

1⁷⁄₁₆"   ⁵⁄₁₆"   ³⁄₄"   ¹⁄₂"

KICKER AND RAIL DETAIL

Center the kicker from side to side.

Make the bearer rail tenons ¹⁄₄" thick × ⁵⁄₈" wide × ¹⁄₂" long.

Notch the bearer rails around the back legs.

Make the bearer rail mortises ⁹⁄₁₆" deep × ¹⁄₄" wide × ⁵⁄₈" long.

Make the kicker tenons ¹⁄₄" thick × ¹⁄₂" wide × ¹⁄₂" long.

Make the kicker mortises ⁹⁄₁₆" deep × ¹⁄₄" wide × ¹⁄₂" long.

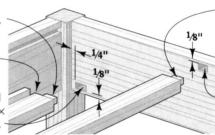

¹⁄₄"   ¹⁄₈"   ¹⁄₈"

LEG TAPERING JIG

LEG BLANK   CUT LINE
29¹⁄₄"
3"   26¹⁄₄"
PLYWOOD   4"
³⁄₈" SPACER   1¹⁄₄"

Photo 1 A simple jig makes short work of tapering the legs on the table saw. Make the jig from a scrap of plywood, as shown in *Leg Tapering Jig.*

Side View on page 101. You can make a tapering jig to help you accomplish this, as shown in **Photo 1.** Sand or plane the sawn edges to smooth them.

5 **Cut the stretcher joinery.** Since the legs have a slight taper, finding the length of the cross rails and fitting them in place can be difficult. The easiest way to do this is to put the table together and mark the pieces directly from the legs.

Clamp the table together securely, and set it on a flat surface such as the top of your table saw. Lay out the location of the stretchers on the legs, as shown in the *Side View.* Clamp the side stretchers to the outside of the legs and mark the shoulder lines, as shown in **Photo 2.** Join the cross rails to the legs with mortise-and-tenon joints, as shown in *Stretcher Detail.* Note that the cross rails and center stretchers only have shoulders on their top and bottom edges. Join the center stretchers to the cross rails with wedged twin tenons, as shown.

6 **Shape the top.** Tilt the blade on your table saw and bevel the underside of the top, as shown in **Photo 3.**

7 **Make the button blocks.** Disassemble the table and rout a ¼-inch groove near the top edge of the side aprons. Rabbet the end of the button block stock, as shown in *Button Block Detail* on page 104, then cut off a 1½-inch-long button. Rabbet and cut until you have four buttons.

8 **Assemble the table.** Put the table back together again, checking to make sure all of the joints fit as they should and that the whole assembly is square. When you are satisfied with the way things fit, take it all apart. Apply glue to the appropriate surfaces, and clamp the table together. After the glue dries, saw the tops of the back legs flush with the tops of the aprons.

STRETCHER DETAIL

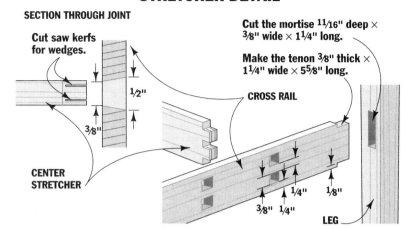

SECTION THROUGH JOINT

Cut saw kerfs for wedges.

½"

⅜"

CENTER STRETCHER

Cut the mortise ¹¹⁄₁₆" deep × ⅜" wide × 1¼" long.

Make the tenon ⅜" thick × 1¼" wide × 5⅝" long.

CROSS RAIL

¼" ⅛"

⅜" ¼"

LEG

Photo 2 **When dealing with very slight angles, such as those involved in fitting a stretcher to a tapered leg, you'll get the best results from marking the piece directly rather than by relying on measurements.**

Photo 3 **Hold the top on edge as you run it past the blade. A tall auxiliary fence screwed to the regular saw fence provides added support.**

Place the top facedown on your bench, and center the leg assembly on it. Fit the button blocks in the grooves in the side aprons, and screw them to the tabletop to secure it.

9 **Cut the drawer joints.** Cut the drawer parts to the sizes in the Materials List on page 101. You can edge glue narrower pieces to make up the bottom, or you can make the bottom from a piece of ¼-inch plywood. Measure the drawer opening and make any necessary adjustments to the dimensions. Join the sides to the front and back with through dovetails, as shown in *Drawer Detail*. Note that the back is narrower than the sides so you can slide the bottom into place after gluing up the drawer box.

10 **Add the drawer bottom.** Cut a groove in the drawer slips, as shown in **Photo 4,** as well as along the bottom edge of the drawer front to hold the drawer bottom. Glue the drawer box together, checking it for square. Rabbet the front and side edges of the drawer bottom to fit the grooves. The grain in the bottom should run from side to side so that the bottom can expand out the back without causing any binding. Slide the bottom in place, and glue it along the drawer front.

11 **Finish up.** Fit the drawer to its opening by hand planing the sides of the box. Once the drawer fits, hold it in place and attach the drawer face with double-sided tape. Remove the drawer and mark the back of the face so you can reposition it. Pry the face free of the box and remove the tape, then glue the face in place.

Chamfer the bottom of the legs slightly. Finish the table with three or four coats of wiping varnish. When the finish dries, attach the pull to the drawer front. As a final touch, rub a little paraffin on the bearer rails to help the drawer glide in and out effortlessly.

BUTTON BLOCK DETAIL

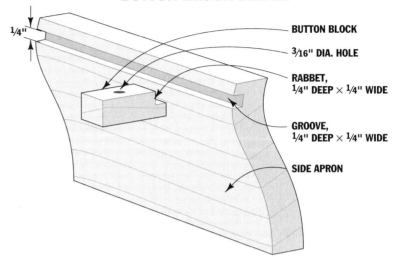

DRAWER DETAIL

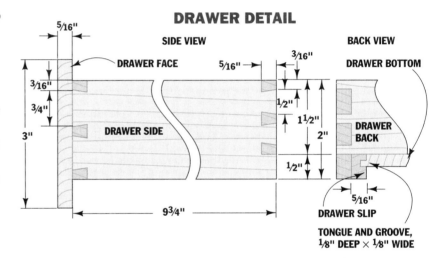

Photo 4 **Using drawer slips is a traditional method of holding the bottom in a drawer. The slips not only reinforce thin drawer sides by thickening the sides where the bottom grooves are cut but they also make the drawer last longer by widening the surfaces on which the drawer slides.**

Design Variations
A Stretched Table

There is a lot of freedom in building occasional tables. Unlike dining tables, where many of the dimensions are predetermined, you can make an occasional table almost any size and shape. This lack of limitations allows you to customize a table to suit a particular look or purpose. It also allows you to adapt the design of an existing table to suit another use.

For example, by shortening the legs of the side table shown

on page 100, you could make it a companion table to a low easy chair. Or by lengthening a few of its parts, you can create an entryway table, as shown here. If you're interested in building this longer version, you can follow the instructions on pages 100–104 with just a few changes.

Obviously, some of the pieces have to be longer. You'll also have to increase the thickness of the lower drawer rail from ½ to ¾ inch so it won't bow. This, in turn,

means you'll need to increase the width of the aprons and the drawer faces by ¼ inch. You should also add ¼ inch to the length of the drawer faces to cover the guide that will run between the drawers. This guide is attached to a center bearer rail, which is tenoned in place.

The drawer boxes are the same size, but you'll need two of them, along with an extra kicker. The dimensions for the parts that change are listed here.

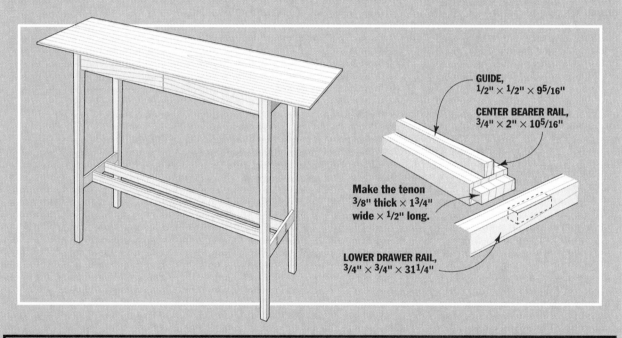

GUIDE, 1/2" × 1/2" × 9⁵/16"

CENTER BEARER RAIL, 3/4" × 2" × 10⁵/16"

Make the tenon 3/8" thick × 1³/4" wide × 1/2" long.

LOWER DRAWER RAIL, 3/4" × 3/4" × 31¹/4"

MATERIALS LIST

PART	QTY.	DIMENSIONS	PART	QTY.	DIMENSIONS
Top	1	¾" × 14" × 38"	Center stretchers	2	⅜" × 1½" × 32⅛"
Upper drawer rail	1	½" × ¾" × 31¼"	Guide	1	½" × ½" × 9⁵/16"
Lower drawer rail	1	¾" × ¾" × 31¼"	Center bearer rail	1	¾" × 2" × 10⁵/16"
Side aprons	2	¾" × 3¼" × 10¾"	Drawer faces	2	⁵/16" × 3¼" × 15¼"
Back apron	1	¾" × 3¼" × 32¼"			

GARDEN BENCH

While there is nothing more complicated than drilling and edge gluing involved in this bench, it has a sophisticated look that belies its construction. You could use similar techniques to build an entire ensemble of outdoor furniture.

In designing outdoor furniture, one of your prime considerations has to be durability. Unless you're willing to slavishly haul your pieces inside to protect them, all aspects of your designs have to be up to the rigors of nature, including the materials you select and the joinery you use.

This little bench is an example of a piece capable of withstanding years of blazing sunshine and driving rain.

It's made of cedar, one of the most naturally rot-resistant species commonly available, and held together with bronze hardware and waterproof glue.

Rather than using a traditional joint like the mortise and tenon to attach the stretcher to the legs, the piece is held in place with bolts. On a piece of outdoor furniture, a mortise-and-tenon joint isn't likely to stay

tight for very long. The wide temperature and humidity swings the piece is apt to see will cause the wood to expand and contract considerably. This movement will gradually loosen a mortise and tenon, opening up gaps for moisture to seep in and eventually causing the wood to rot. A bolted joint can easily be tightened should it become loose, and it has fewer places for moisture to hide.

EXPLODED VIEW

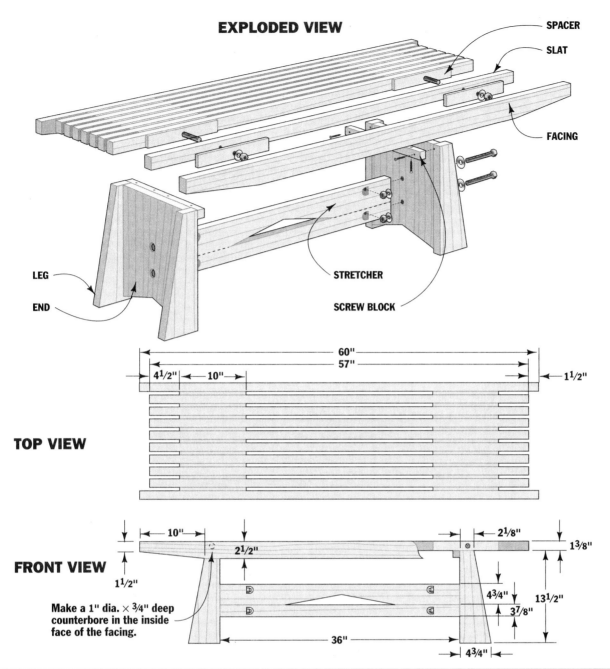

SPACER

SLAT

FACING

LEG

END

STRETCHER

SCREW BLOCK

TOP VIEW

60"
57"
4½"
10"
1½"

FRONT VIEW

10"
2½"
2⅛"
1⅜"
1½"
13½"
4¾"
3⅞"
36"
4¾"

Make a 1" dia. × ¾" deep counterbore in the inside face of the facing.

MATERIALS LIST				
PART	**QTY.**	**DIMENSIONS**	**HARDWARE**	**QTY.**
Slats	8	1¼" × 1⅜" × 57"	⁵⁄₁₆" × 15" threaded rods	2
Spacers	18	½" × 1⅜" × 10"	⁵⁄₁₆" washers	4
Facings	2	1¼" × 2½" × 60"	⁵⁄₁₆" nuts	4
Ends	2	1½" × 12" × 13"	⁵⁄₁₆" × 5" bronze hex cap screws (bolts)*	4
Legs	4	1¼" × 4¾" × 13½"	⁵⁄₁₆" bronze flat washers*	8
Stretcher	1 (2 pieces)	1¼" × 1¾" × 36" 1¼" × 3" × 36"	⁵⁄₁₆" bronze nuts*	4
Screw blocks	2	1" × 1" × 14"	#8 × 1¾" bronze round-head wood screws*	16
			Resorcinol glue or epoxy	
			*Available from Jamestown Distributors: (800) 423-0030.	

Procedure

1 Cut the parts to size. The parts for this bench can be cut from five 10-foot cedar 2 × 4s, as shown in *Parts Layout.* Rip the slats, spacers, and facings to size, leaving them slightly oversized in thickness. Plane them to final thickness according to the Materials List on page 107. Cut the parts for the legs and ends, as shown, and edge glue the pieces to make up the necessary widths. Cut the two pieces for the stretcher about ¼ inch too long, and set them aside until later.

2 Make the bench top. Drill holes through the spacers and near both ends of the slats, as shown in *Hole Detail* and in **Photo 1.** Draw lines across the top of the slats to help you in positioning the spacers. Glue the spacers and the slats together, as shown in the *Top View* on page 107.

Slip the threaded rods through the holes, and fasten them in place with washers and nuts. Before the glue dries, carefully align the ends of the spacers as well as the ends of the slats and the top surfaces of all of the pieces. Tighten the nuts to squeeze the joints closed. If necessary, add clamps to bring the pieces together snugly.

3 Add the facings. Band-saw the ends of the facings to taper them, as shown in the *Front View* on page 107. Clean up the sawn edges with a plane or by sanding them. Counterbore the inside surfaces to fit over the ends of the threaded rod, then glue the facings to the rest of the top. After the glue has dried, use a hand plane or belt sander to smooth the entire top surface.

4 Make the leg assemblies. Make the angled cuts on the bottom of the ends, as shown in the *End View,* and taper the legs, as shown

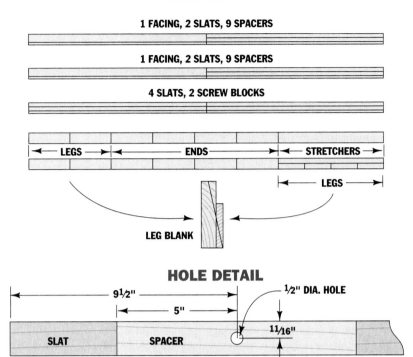

PARTS LAYOUT

1 FACING, 2 SLATS, 9 SPACERS

1 FACING, 2 SLATS, 9 SPACERS

4 SLATS, 2 SCREW BLOCKS

◄— LEGS —► ◄— ENDS —► ◄— STRETCHERS —►

◄— LEGS —►

LEG BLANK

HOLE DETAIL

9½"

5"

½" DIA. HOLE

11/16"

SLAT   SPACER

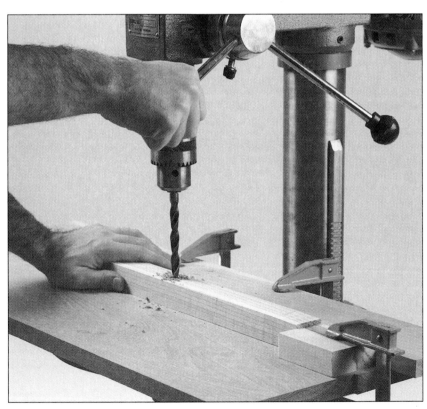

Photo 1 **A fence and a stop block help make short work of drilling the holes for the threaded rod through the slats and spacers. The holes are purposely oversized to allow room for alignment as you glue up.**

in the *Front View,* on the band saw. Sand or plane the sawn edges smooth. Glue the legs to the sides of the ends.

5 Make the stretcher. Make the angled cuts in the wider of the two pieces you set aside for the stretcher, as shown in *Stretcher and Screw Block Detail.* Sand the sawn edges smooth, then glue the two pieces together to form the stretcher. Trim the stretcher to length after the glue dries.

6 Drill the bolt holes. Drill and counterbore ⁵⁄₁₆-inch holes for the bolts in the leg assemblies, as shown in the *End View.* Hold the stretcher vertically in a vise, and align one leg assembly on top of it, as shown in **Photo 2.** Drill two holes about 1 inch deep into the end of the stretcher, using the holes in the leg assembly as a guide. Set the leg assembly aside, and drill the holes in the stretcher to their full depth. Repeat the process on the other end of the stretcher.

Note: Make sure you hold the leg assemblies in their proper orientation. It would be easy to get mixed up and hold one upside down.

7 Make the nut holes. Drill 1-inch holes through the stretcher to hold the nuts, as shown in *Stretcher and Screw Block Detail.* Finish the D-shaped cutouts with a coping saw.

8 Assemble the bench. With the bench top upside down on your workbench, hold the leg assemblies in place and bolt them to the stretcher. Drill holes through the screw blocks, as shown in *Stretcher and Screw Block Detail.* Attach the screw blocks to both the leg assemblies and the bench top with round-head wood screws. Drill pilot holes first to prevent the wood from splitting.

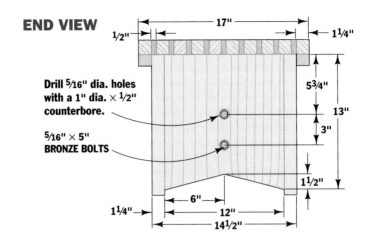

END VIEW

Drill ⁵⁄₁₆" dia. holes with a 1" dia. × ¹⁄₂" counterbore.

⁵⁄₁₆" × 5" BRONZE BOLTS

17"   1¹⁄₄"   ¹⁄₂"   5³⁄₄"   13"   3"   1¹⁄₂"   1¹⁄₄"   6"   12"   14¹⁄₂"

STRETCHER AND SCREW BLOCK DETAIL

1" DIA. D-SHAPED HOLES

STRETCHER

18"   1¹⁄₂"   3"   1³⁄₄"   GLUE LINE   SCREW BLOCK

7⁄8"   4"   16¹⁄₂"   ³⁄₁₆" DIA. HOLES   1"   4"   1⁵⁄₈"   4"

Photo 2 **An extra set of hands helps a lot when you're using the leg assembly to locate the holes in the end of the stretcher.**

9 Finish up. While the bench is still upside down, chamfer the bottoms of the legs slightly to keep them from splitting should the bench slide on the ground. What kind of finish to apply is up to you. If you want to preserve the color and look of the fresh cedar, wipe on a penetrating finish such as what you would use for cedar siding on a house. Then reapply the finish every other year or so. Or you can simply allow the bench to weather naturally. Left alone, the wood will turn a beautiful silvery gray.

GEAR BOX

You'll find many uses for this easy-to-assemble pine gear box, from hauling camping gear to storing your outside Christmas lights from year to year. Strong and simple joinery ensure that your grandkids will get good use out of it as well.

The small proportions of this pine chest make it more versatile, not less. It's rugged enough for outdoor use—hauling camping gear or toting tools around the yard. Indoors, at the foot of a child's bed, for example, it could house blankets, sweaters, or toys. It makes a perfect kid's-height seat as well. The handles make it portable even for a young child, so it can be put into service as a game table, a treasure chest—whatever a young

imagination dreams up. You could easily enlarge the dimensions, keeping the same design, and end up with an attractive, full-sized blanket chest.

You can make the gear box from just a single 12-foot length of 1 × 12 clear pine. If you're going to paint the box, you could use less-expensive #1 pine. Either way, leave the inside unfinished, and the natural pine scent will last for years. Using 1 × 12 stock eliminates the

need for planing to thickness and edge gluing. If you choose a hardwood, plan on getting about 15 board feet of rough stock.

The handles are glued onto the sides after the box is assembled, so cutting the box joints is straightforward. The edge of the bottom is rabbeted, and the tongue rests in a groove cut around the four sides of the box. The lid is a framed panel. All told, it's a basic box made with strong but simple joinery.

EXPLODED VIEW

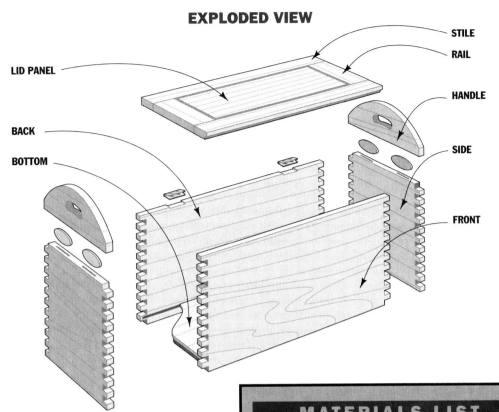

STILE

RAIL

LID PANEL

HANDLE

BACK

SIDE

BOTTOM

FRONT

TOP VIEW

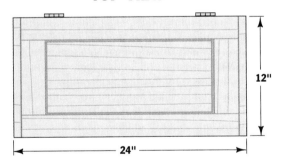

12"

24"

MATERIALS LIST

PART	QTY.	DIMENSIONS
Sides	2	$\frac{3}{4}" \times 11" \times 12"$
Front and back	2	$\frac{3}{4}" \times 11" \times 24"$
Handles	2	$\frac{3}{4}" \times 3\frac{3}{4}" \times 12"$
Bottom	1	$\frac{3}{4}" \times 11" \times 23"$
Lid stiles	2	$\frac{3}{4}" \times 2\frac{1}{4}" \times 22\frac{3}{8}"$
Lid rails	2	$\frac{3}{4}" \times 2\frac{1}{4}" \times 10"$
Lid panel	1	$\frac{3}{4}" \times 8" \times 18\frac{1}{2}"$

HARDWARE

$1\frac{1}{2}"$ brass butt hinges and screws	1 pair	

FRONT VIEW

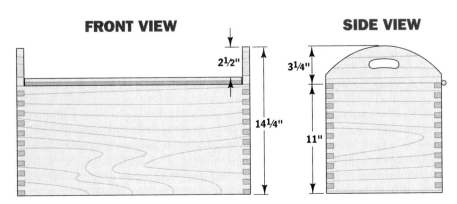

$2\frac{1}{2}"$

$14\frac{1}{4}"$

SIDE VIEW

$3\frac{1}{4}"$

11"

Procedure

1 **Cut the pieces to size.** Cut the parts to the sizes in the Materials List on page 111, but leave the lid stiles a couple of inches long to allow for the horns on either end. The lid panel and the bottom are narrower than you might expect to allow for expansion.

2 **Cut the box joints.** Set up a dado blade on your table saw or a straight bit in your table-mounted router, and cut the corner joints with a box joint jig. Make the fingers exactly ½ inch wide. Mark the top edge of each piece, then start cutting with the marked edge toward the jig's pin. This will help you orient the pieces correctly.

3 **Cut the groove for the bottom.** The groove runs straight through the sides, but you need to stop it on the front and back, as shown in *Bottom Groove Detail.* Cut the groove with a ¼-inch straight bit in a table-mounted router. Mark the bit location on the table and fence, and mark the ends of the grooves on the front and back, as shown in **Photo 1** and **Photo 2.**

4 **Rabbet the bottom.** Cut a ⅜-inch-deep × ½-inch-wide rabbet into the underside of the bottom to form a ¼-inch-thick tongue. It should fit snugly, but not tightly, in the groove.

5 **Glue up the box.** Spread glue on the fingers and push the joints together. Working one corner at a time, slip the bottom in place before assembling the final joints. Use clamps to tighten the joints, but once everything is seated, remove them. Measure the diagonals of the box for squareness.

6 **Cut and shape the handle.** Lay out the handle shape on the handle blanks, as shown in *Handle Detail.* Drill the ends of the cutout with a ⅞-inch Forstner bit, then connect the holes

BOTTOM GROOVE DETAIL

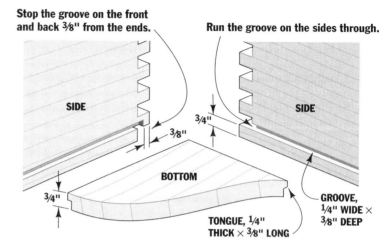

Stop the groove on the front and back ⅜" from the ends.

Run the groove on the sides through.

SIDE

SIDE

¾"

⅜"

BOTTOM

¾"

GROOVE, ¼" WIDE × ⅜" DEEP

TONGUE, ¼" THICK × ⅜" LONG

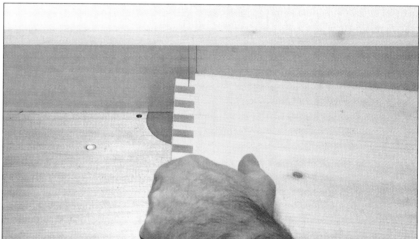

Photo 1 Carefully lay the workpiece onto the bit so the groove stop mark is aligned with the left bit mark.

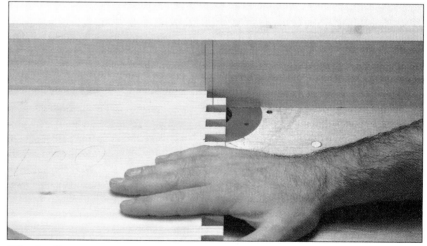

Photo 2 Then stop the cut when the right bit mark is aligned with the stop mark at the other end of the groove.

with a saber saw. Cut the arc in the top of the handles, and save the cutoffs for clamping cauls. Sand the sawn edges. Glue and clamp the handles to the sides, as shown in **Photo 3.**

7 **Rout the mortises.** Lay out the mortises in the lid stiles with a mortise gauge, as shown in *Lid Joinery Detail.* With a plunge router, rout the four mortises. Chisel the ends square.

8 **Cut the tenons.** First make the shoulder cuts in the faces of the rails. Guide the pieces through the table saw with the miter gauge, and use a stop block along the rip fence to determine the tenon length. Adjust the blade and make the shoulder cuts in the edges of the rails. Finally, cut the tenon cheeks using a tenoning fixture.

9 **Cut the groove for the lid panel.** Cut the lid groove with a ¼-inch straight bit in a table-mounted router. Position the fence so the groove is in the middle of the stock, and set the depth of cut to ½ inch.

10 **Fit the lid panel.** The edges of the panel are rabbeted on both sides to form a tongue that fits into the grooves in the frame pieces. Cut the rabbets on the router table.

11 **Assemble and attach the lid.** Glue the lid frame together, with the panel in place. After the glue has cured, cut away the horns; trim the ends of the lid, so it fits between the handles with a ¹⁄₁₆-inch gap at each end. Rout a cove on the lid's front bottom edge to make opening the box easier. Cut the mor-tises for the hinges and attach the lid.

12 **Apply a finish.** If your gear box will see hard use, a durable finish like paint is in order. This gear box was finished with milk paint, which maintains a slightly weathered, yet attractive appearance, despite years of use.

HANDLE DETAIL

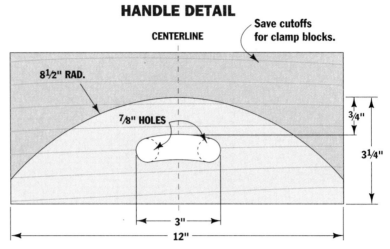

Save cutoffs for clamp blocks.

CENTERLINE

8½" RAD.

⅞" HOLES

¾"

3¼"

3"

12"

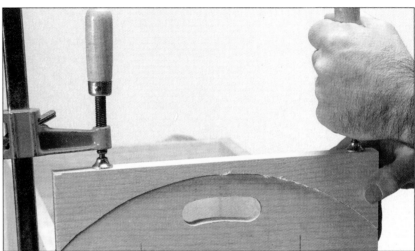

Photo 3 Use the curved cutoffs from the handles as clamping blocks when you glue the handles in place. A couple of biscuits in each joint will help keep the pieces aligned.

LID JOINERY DETAIL

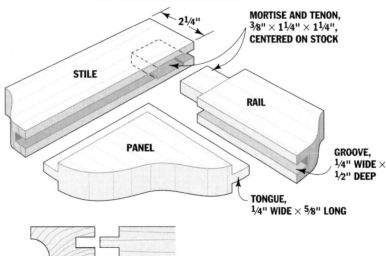

2¼"

STILE

PANEL

RAIL

MORTISE AND TENON, ⅜" × 1¼" × 1¼", CENTERED ON STOCK

GROOVE, ¼" WIDE × ½" DEEP

TONGUE, ¼" WIDE × ⅝" LONG

STUDY DESK

Students, teachers, artists, writers, and readers alike will find that this tabletop desk increases their comfort and productivity. It combines a large angled desk surface with a book stand. The shallow drawer underneath is just right for stowing paper and pencils.

If you've ever worked with a reference book, a notepad, and a spreadsheet all at the same time, you know how frustrating it can be to juggle everything back and forth. Your neck and eyes strain as your focus constantly changes. You're constantly flipping from one thing to the next until you've lost your pen and spilled your coffee.

This desk will put an end to all of that. It's designed to help you keep your papers and books orga-nized while you're using them. The desktop is angled to make writing, drawing, or simple note taking much easier. At the same time, the book stand holds reference materials in the best position for reading. Use the desk wherever it's most convenient. The rubber feet make it friendly even to that most common of workplaces, the dining room table. Make one for yourself, or make up a batch for all of your favorite paper-pushers.

The desk is easier to build than its assorted angles might suggest. The desk itself is just a panel with two more panels mortised into it from underneath to make legs. The joinery is all at right angles, and the slant comes from the way the bottom of the legs are cut. The drawer is held together with box joints. And the book stand is a three-part assembly employing nothing more complicated than a splined miter joint.

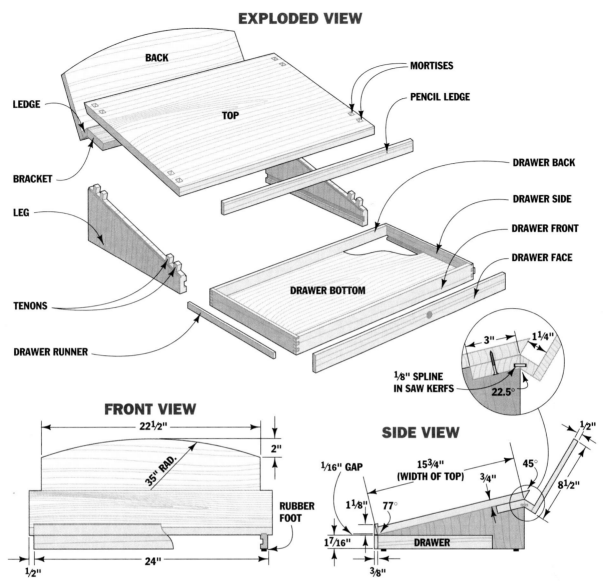

EXPLODED VIEW

BACK

MORTISES

LEDGE

PENCIL LEDGE

TOP

BRACKET

DRAWER BACK

DRAWER SIDE

LEG

DRAWER FRONT

DRAWER FACE

TENONS

DRAWER BOTTOM

DRAWER RUNNER

1/8" SPLINE IN SAW KERFS

3" 1 1/4"

22.5°

FRONT VIEW

22 1/2"

2"

35" RAD.

RUBBER FOOT

24"

1/2"

SIDE VIEW

1/2"

1/16" GAP

15 3/4" (WIDTH OF TOP)

45°

3/4"

8 1/2"

1 1/8"

77°

DRAWER

1 7/16"

3/8"

MATERIALS LIST

PART	QTY.	DIMENSIONS
Top*	1	$3/4" \times 15\,3/4" \times 25"$
Legs*	2	$3/4" \times 16\,5/8" \times 9"$
Wedges	8	$1/8" \times 1/2" \times 3/4"$
Pencil ledge**	1	$3/8" \times 1\,1/8" \times 24"$
Drawer sides	2	$5/16" \times 1\,7/16" \times 12"$
Drawer front	1	$5/16" \times 1\,7/16" \times 22\,7/16"$
Drawer back	1	$5/16" \times 15/16" \times 22\,7/16"$
Drawer bottom	1	$1/4" \times 11\,7/8" \times 22"$
Drawer face**	1	$3/8" \times 1\,7/16" \times 24"$
Drawer runners	2	$1/4" \times 1/2" \times 12"$
Bracket	1	$3/4" \times 3" \times 22\,1/2"$

PART	QTY.	DIMENSIONS
Ledge	1	$3/4" \times 1\,1/4" \times 22\,1/2"$
Back	1	$1/2" \times 8\,1/2" \times 22\,1/2"$

HARDWARE

#6 × 3/4" flat-head wood screws	2
#4 × 1/2" flat-head wood screws	2
1/2" brass knob	1
#6 × 1 1/4" flat-head wood screws	8
1/2" dia. rubber feet	4

*Make a single, glued-up 17" × 36" panel.

**Make from a single piece, ripped lengthwise.

Procedure

1 Cut the parts to size. All of the desk parts are solid wood except for the drawer bottom, which is ¼-inch plywood. The desk shown is made of cherry. Cut the pieces except for the top and the legs to the sizes in the Materials List on page 115. For the best appearance, rip the drawer face and the pencil ledge from the same board so the grain is continuous on both pieces.

2 Glue up stock for the top and legs. Edge join boards to make a 17-inch-wide × 36-inch-long panel. Plane the boards to a final thickness of ¾ inch before gluing up, then take care to keep them flat when clamping.

3 Make the top. Crosscut the panel to separate the leg blank from the top. Leave both parts long for now. Rip the back edge of the top at a 45 degree angle and the front edge at 77 degrees, as shown in the *Side View* on page 115. Round over the top edge with a plane. Crosscut the top to length.

Lay out the mortises, as shown in *Mortise-and-Tenon Layout.* Drill ⅜-inch holes at the center of each mortise. Then cut ½-inch-wide × ⅛-inch-deep dadoes across the underside of the top, as shown. Cutting the dadoes after drilling wipes out any tearout from the drill. Pare the mortises to square them from both sides.

4 Make the tenons. Straighten the edges of the leg blank that will receive the tenons. Although you'll be crosscutting the wood, use the rip fence on the table saw to trim these two edges. Note: It's not necessary that the blank be square, only that the edges be straight. Make a diagonal cut in the waste area between the legs to separate them, as shown in *Leg Layout.*

RIPPINGS

THE RUBBED JOINT

If you use old-style hot hide glue, it's possible to glue up an edge joint without clamps. The procedure is the same as described on page 26, except the glue goes on hot as coffee. It's quite runny when hot, but it gels rapidly as it cools. As the glue cools, you squeeze and squish the joint together while rubbing each board into position. When the glue gels, it grabs tight. Old-timers call this a rubbed joint.

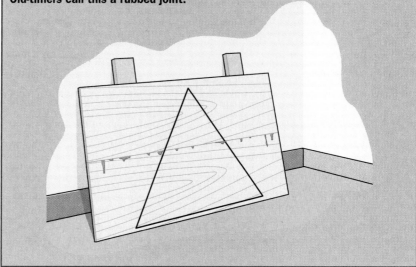

MORTISE-AND-TENON LAYOUT

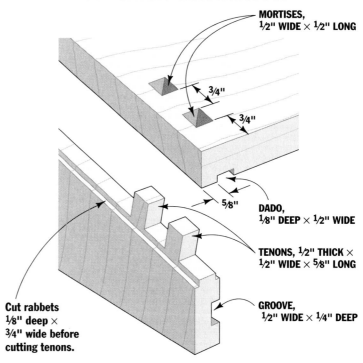

MORTISES, ½" WIDE × ½" LONG

¾"

¾"

5/8"

DADO, ⅛" DEEP × ½" WIDE

TENONS, ½" THICK × ½" WIDE × 5/8" LONG

GROOVE, ½" WIDE × ¼" DEEP

Cut rabbets ⅛" deep × ¾" wide before cutting tenons.

With a table-mounted router, rabbet both sides of the leg blanks, as shown in *Mortise-and-Tenon Layout.* The resulting ½-inch-thick tongue must fit snugly in the dado. Start with the rabbet a little less than ⅛ inch deep, and raise the bit very slightly, shaving both sides until the fit is just right. Insert the legs into the dadoes, so there is an even amount of excess at both ends. Mark the end cuts on the leg at the edges of the top, and mark the tenons through the mortises, as shown in **Photo 1.**

Extend the tenon layout marks down to the shoulders of the rabbets with a sharp pencil. Saw down these lines with a tenon saw to within about ⅛ inch of the shoulders. Use a coping saw to cut away the wood between the tenons to leave the tongue a little less than ⅛ inch long. Test the fit of the tenons in their mortises.

5 Shape the legs. Table-saw the front and back edges of the legs at an angle, as shown in *Leg Layout.* Guide the pieces with the miter gauge. Lay out the bottom edge of the legs by measuring 5 inches along the back of the leg

and 1½ inches along the front of the leg from the edge of the rabbet. Connect the marks with a line, and cut on the band saw. Plane the bottom edges straight.

Cut the groove for the drawer runner on the inside surface of each leg, as shown in *Mortise-and-Tenon Layout,* with a dado cutter. Guide the pieces through the cut with their bottom edges against the rip fence.

6 Attach the legs. Make two saw kerfs in each tenon, as shown in *Wedge Detail.* Taper the wedges at a 1:8 slope. Widen the mortises to match. Glue and clamp the legs to the top. Spread glue on the wedges and tap them into the kerfs to lock the joint together. When the glue dries, trim the wedges flush to the top of the tenons.

Photo 1 Reach through the mortises with a sharp awl to mark the tenons. While the legs are in position, also mark for the end cuts at the edges of the top.

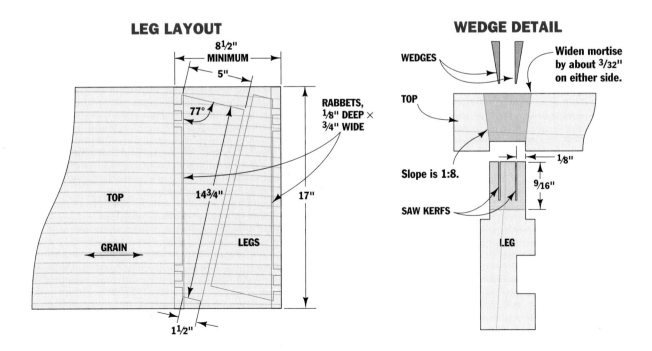

LEG LAYOUT

8½"
MINIMUM

5"

77°

RABBETS,
⅛" DEEP ×
¾" WIDE

TOP

14¾"

17"

GRAIN

LEGS

1½"

WEDGE DETAIL

WEDGES

Widen mortise by about 3/32" on either side.

TOP

Slope is 1:8.

SAW KERFS

⅛"

9/16"

LEG

7 Attach the pencil ledge. Bevel the top edge of the pencil ledge, then glue it in place, as shown in **Photo 2.**

8 Make the drawer. Join the drawer parts with ¼-inch box joints, as shown in *Drawer Detail.* Note that the drawer back stops just above the drawer bottom, allowing you to slide the bottom in after glue-up.

Rout a ¼-inch groove along the inside of the drawer sides and front for the bottom. Don't worry that the groove comes through the drawer front—the drawer face will cover it. Glue up the drawer, making sure you keep it square. When the glue dries, slide the drawer bottom in place, and fasten it to the drawer back with ¾-inch wood screws. Fasten the runners to the drawer sides with ½-inch screws, and slide the drawer into place. Glue the drawer face on the drawer box, aligning the grain with that of the pencil ledge. Screw the brass knob to the drawer face.

9 Make the book stand. The book stand is a three-part assembly that is screwed to the underside of the top. Make the bracket/ledge assembly by joining the two pieces with a spline miter. As shown in the *Side View* on page 115, the miter angle is 22.5 degrees, but don't worry about being so exact. Close to that is fine. The pieces are small enough that you can glue them without adding separate clamping blocks, as shown in **Photo 3.** Cut and sand the arc on the book-stand back. Then glue and screw the back to the ledge. Screw the assembled book stand to the underside of the top.

10 Finish up. Disassemble the desk as much as possible. Finish the desk with a durable finish. The one shown was given four coats of a wiping varnish, then it was rubbed to a satin sheen with #0000 steel wool.

Photo 2 Place a 2 × 4 along the back of the desk to give the clamps something to grip as you glue the pencil ledge in place.

DRAWER DETAIL

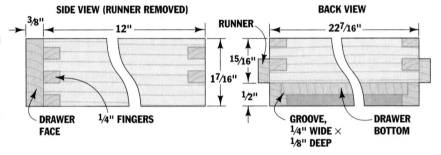

SIDE VIEW (RUNNER REMOVED)   BACK VIEW

3/8"   12"   RUNNER   22 7/16"

15/16"

1 7/16"

1/2"

DRAWER FACE   1/4" FINGERS   GROOVE, 1/4" WIDE × 1/8" DEEP   DRAWER BOTTOM

Photo 3 The ledge and the bracket are narrow enough that you can apply pressure directly across the joint without adding separate clamping blocks. Apply pressure gently so you don't crush the edges.

INDEX

Note: Page references in *italic* indicate illustrations. **Boldface** references indicate photographs.

B

Band saw
    cutting curves with, 32–33, *33*, **33**
    cutting tenons with, 52, *52*, **52**
    ripping with, 17
Bevel, sliding, 11, *11*
Biscuit joiner, 29, 39, **39**, *64*, 65
Biscuit joints
    assembling, 64
    butt, 83, *83*
    edge-to-edge, 28, *28*, 29
    for joining rails and stiles, 64–65, *64*
    mitered, 39, *39*, 71, *71*, 96–97
    for sheet goods, 39, *39*
Blade guard, 16
Bolted rail joints, 70, *70*
Box joints, *81*, 84, *84*–85
Breadboard ends, 76, *76*
Bridle joints, 70, *70*
Butt joints, *81*, 83, *83*

C

Caliper, dial, 11, **29**
Case joints, overview of, 80, **80,** *81*. See *also specific types*
Clamp cart project, 40, **40,** *41*
Clamping
    dovetail joints, 89, *89*
    edge-to-edge joints, 21, 26–27, *27*
    face-to-face joints, 35
    facts about, 35
    loose tenon joints, 62–63, *63*
    miters, 38–39, *38*
    rabbet-and-groove joints, 38, *38*
    right angle joints, 36, *36*
    wedged joints, 61, *61*
Crosscut box, *18*
Crosscutting, 17, 18
Cross-half joints, 68, *68*
Cupping of boards, 23, *23*
Curved lines
    band-sawing, 32–33, *33*, **33**
    creating with mitered shoulder joints, 75, *75*
    for edge-to-edge joints, 32, *32*
Cutting board, 55
Cutting gauge, 54, *54*

D

Dadoes. *See* Housings
Dovetail joints
    assembling, 88–89, **88**
    clamping, 89, *89*
    double-lap, *81*, 92, *92*
    gluing, 89, *89*
    jigs for, 93, **93**
    laying out, 85, *85*, 86, **89**
    making the pins, 88, *88*, 89
    making the tails, 86–87, *87*, 89
    mitered shoulder, *81*, 90, *90*, **90**
    mock, 71, *71*, *81*, 97, *97*
    problem solving for, 98
    secret mitered, *81*, 92, *92*
    single-lap (half-blind), 69, *69*, *81*, 90–91, *91*
    sliding, 95, *95*
Dovetail keys, 71, *71*, *81*, 97, *97*
Dowel joints, 63, *63*, 83
Drawboring, 65
Drill press, 49, 82, 83

E

Edge-to-edge joints. *See also specific types*
    aligning, 28–29, *28*, *29*
    avoiding pith in, 21, *21*
    with biscuits, 28, *28*, 29
    choosing boards for, 22–23
    clamping, 21, 26–27, *27*
    cleaning up glue line on, 27
    on curved lines, 32–33, *32*
    with dowels, 29
    fine-tuning, 27
    gluing, 20–21, 26, *26*
    grain direction in, 5, **20,** 21, *21*
    jointing edges for, 24–25, *24*, *25*
    marking, 21, *21*
    problem solving for, 30
    with splines, 28–29, *28*, **28**
    strength of, 20–21, *20*
    veneer inserts in, 31, *31*, **31**, 32
    wood movement and, 20, *20*
Exposed joinery, **2,** 3, 5

F

Face edge, jointing, *12*, 13
Face side, jointing, 12
Face-to-face joints, 34–35, *34*, **35**
Feather keys, 71, *71*, *81*, 97, *97*

G

Fence, auxiliary, 16
Finger joints. *See* Box joints

G

Garden bench project, 106–9, **106,** *107*, *108*, **108,** *109*, **109**
Gear box project, 110–13, **110,** *111*, *112*, **112,** *113*, **113**
Gluing
    dovetail joints, 89, *89*
    edge-to-edge joints, 20–21, 26, *26*
    face-to-face joints, 34, 35, **35**
    long-grain right angles, 36
    loose tenon joints, 62–63
    mortise-and-tenon joints, 53
    rabbet joints, *38*
Grain direction, 4–5, *4*, **20,** 21, *21*

H

Half-lap joints, 68–69, *69*
Haunched joints, 74, *74*
Housings, 94, *94*, **94**

J

Jigs and fixtures
    for biscuit joiner, *64*, 65
    box joint, 84, *84*
    dovetail, 93, **93**
    feather key, 71, **71**
    leg tapering, *102*, **102**
    mortising, 47, *47*, 62
    tenoning, 51, *51*, **51**
Joiner's mallet, 55, *55*
Joinery
    configuration overview, 5, *5*
    defined, 2
Jointer knives, 15, *15*
Jointer plane, 25
Jointing
    face edge, *12*, 13
    face side, 12
    for glue-up, 24, *24*
    with hand tools, 25, *25*
    with a router, 13, *13*
    on a table saw, 24
    technique for, 14, *14*, 30, *30*

K

Knock-down joints, 60, **60**